What Leaders Are Saying

"Bishop Jackson blows a trumpet in our ears with his new book, *The Way of the Warrior*. Its timeless truths assemble an achievable way for all of us to more effectively walk out our lives in productivity and insightfulness."

Bishop T. D. Jakes Sr., founding pastor,
The Potter's House, Dallas

"Your outlook will determine your outcome and your choice of weapons will determine your effectiveness in warfare. Harry Jackson Jr. knows these principles well and shapes a winner's attitude in *The Way of the Warrior*. Be prepared for your next battle by reading this valuable manual!"

James W. Goll, cofounder, Encounters Network

"*The Way of the Warrior* by Harry Jackson is a book after my own heart. Very few books integrate warfare and transformation as well as this one does. Transformation causes society to reflect God's Kingdom plan. Romans 8 says that our minds are at enmity with God. If you want to read a book that will cause your mind to think the way God is thinking today, then *The Way of the Warrior* is for you!"

Dr. Chuck D. Pierce, president, Glory of Zion International
Ministries, Inc.; vice president, Global Harvest Ministries

"The promises of God are unattainable without possessing an overcomer's heart; those who overcome inherit God's rewards. Bishop Jackson's voice is a trumpet; his wisdom is a weapon.

This book has an anointing on it that will empower spiritual warriors in their battles."

Francis Frangipane, senior pastor, River of Life Ministries

"Harry Jackson is a man of impeccable character. He knows what it means to persevere, to overcome hardship, to achieve excellence. A degree from Harvard qualifies him in this temporal world; his achievements on spiritual battlefields qualify him in the Kingdom without end."

from the foreword by the Rev. Tommy Tenney,
GodChasers.Network

"My friend Bishop Harry Jackson's book *The Way of the Warrior* is a powerful training manual for believers serious about impacting their sphere of influence with Spirit-led 'weaponry' and Word-inspired 'tactics.' Champions for God who are passionate about fulfilling their destiny and becoming world-class warrior-leaders will be challenged to press toward their high calling."

John Bevere, Messenger International

"It is my pleasure to commend to you Bishop Harry Jackson's new book, *The Way of the Warrior*. This book is a must-read for anyone who wants a cutting-edge strategy to accomplish God's will in these last days."

Marcus D. Lamb, president/CEO, Daystar Television Network

"Like a jeweler placing a fine stone into a new ring, Bishop Harry Jackson Jr. has taken something as familiar yet precious as the life of David and placed it into a setting that allows it to reflect a new dimension of brilliance. *The Way of the Warrior* will enable a rising generation to become familiar with the principles that helped David achieve greatness, and it will empower them as well."

Rod Parsley, senior pastor, World Harvest Church,
Columbus, Ohio

The Way of the Warrior

How to Fulfill Life's Most Difficult Assignments

Harry R. Jackson Jr.

Chosen
Grand Rapids, Michigan

© 2005 by Harry R. Jackson Jr.

Published by Chosen Books
a division of Baker Publishing Group
P.O. Box 6287, Grand Rapids, MI 49516-6287
www.chosenbooks.com

Printed in the United States of America

Library of Congress Cataloging-in-Publication Data
Jackson, Harry R.
     The way of the warrior : how to fulfill life's most difficult assign-
ments / Harry R. Jackson, Jr.
          p.   cm.
     Includes bibliographical references and index.
     ISBN 0-8007-9401-X (pbk.)
     1. David, King of Israel. 2. Spiritual warfare. 3. War—Religious as-
pects—Christianity. 4. Christian life. I. Title.
BS580.D3J33 2005
248.4—dc22   2005013297

This book is lovingly dedicated to Arthur D. Wright, Esq. He walked "the way of the warrior" until his untimely death just ten days before this book was finished. Arthur was only 47 when he died, but he gave the world a tremendous gift. He left a legacy—his example. Arthur lived the message I espouse in these pages. He ministered to scores of people through his law practice. In addition, through his role as a deacon, he touched multitudes. I will remember him most as a valued friend, trusted advisor and intercessor whom I loved. As David loved Jonathan, so was my love for this man and for the principles he lived. He lived well, he loved well, he died well. May all who read this book follow suit!

Contents

Foreword

I can think of no better story to illustrate the life of a warrior—complete with its failures and recoveries, devastating defeats and glorious victories—than the life of David. David's life exemplified the ultimate aim of every warrior—to survive; and beyond survival, to thrive.

I can think of no better friend than Harry Jackson. Most times a book is recommended for content only. This book certainly has content to impact your life. I must also take this opportunity, however, to recommend both the writing and the writer. Harry Jackson is a man of impeccable character. He knows what it means to persevere, to overcome hardship, to achieve excellence. A degree from Harvard qualifies him in this temporal world; his achievements on spiritual battlefields qualify him in the Kingdom without end.

Harry Jackson and *The Way of the Warrior*—both highly recommended by Tommy Tenney and both anointed by God.

The Reverend Tommy Tenney,
GodChasers.Network

Acknowledgments

This book has been a labor of love, for which I thank our Lord and Savior for allowing me to pen. Next, I thank Jane Campbell for her undying vision for this book. She and the people at Chosen/Baker have been the best. Special kudos goes to my editor, Ann Weinheimer, who went the extra mile to ensure we completed the manuscript. Jan Sherman has once again put in a yeoman's effort without which these words would never have been published. Last but not least, I thank my family, Michele, Joni and Elizabeth, for sharing me with the world.

1

Collision Course

Is Your Head in the Game?

War must be carried on systematically, and to do it you must have men of character activated by principles of honor.

General George Washington

Shots rang out in an Atlanta courtroom on March 11, 2005. In just a few brief moments, three people including the judge lay dead, a dangerous man was on the loose leaving a trail of violence behind him and an innocent woman was swept into a nightmarish ordeal. Police fanned out quickly in a massive multistate manhunt, vowing to catch this man at all costs. But gunman Brian Nichols would not be nabbed by high-tech investigative gadgets or shrewd police work. He would surrender, instead, to the power of compassion and love.

To the world's surprise, the Christian woman whom Nichols abducted in a parking lot and held hostage in her own apartment talked him into ending his violent rampage. She was not a preacher, a Bible scholar or even a "super" Christian (whatever that is). Ashley Smith was just a woman on her own personal journey with Christ. And this single mom's response to her abductor demonstrates the power each of us has to change our world. Her life was suddenly on a collision course with destruction, but, confronting her fear with faith, she chose to take courageous action. In other words, she kept her head in the game. Let's take a look at how she did it.

Ashley happened to be reading *The Purpose-Driven Life* by Rick Warren. Securing permission to read to her captor from the book, she turned to the two Scriptures given for that day's reading. These words gave both Smith and Nichols a ray of hope in a seemingly hopeless situation.

The first Scripture declared that greatness is accessed by servanthood. It reads: "Whoever wants to be great must become a servant" (Mark 10:43, MESSAGE). Ashley Smith must have embraced this verse because, with a servant's heart, she was able to speak to the deep needs of the desperate man who held her hostage. She served him the Word of God, like a friend bringing a cup of cool water to someone parched in the desert.

The next verse was also important. It said that someone is judged by what he or she does (see Matthew 7:16). Like Ashley, Brian Nichols must have taken this Scripture to heart as well. The chapter offered further hope that he could find purpose in an otherwise ruined life. Although both people had difficult choices before them, Ashley's wise actions may have saved many lives.

She became the voice of reason and, in a strange way, a prophetic voice from God. Perhaps she spoke with such conviction because of her own personal struggles. Looking at her own life, she could have no doubt found reasons for anger, reasons to be discouraged and reasons to give up on herself and others. We all can. But, drawing strength from both the Scriptures and the power of Christ, she acted courageously and decided not to try to escape but to influence a man whom others might have considered past hope.

This incident came at a vulnerable time for Ashley Smith. Just four years earlier, her husband had been murdered in an altercation near their home. He died in her arms, in fact. Can you imagine having to wash your dead husband's blood off your body after feeling his life slip away? Events like these can leave terrible, unanswered questions for those left behind, like Ashley.

More difficult events followed the death of her husband, but at the time of her abduction, she was finally beginning to get back on her feet, beginning to dream again. She could have felt as though her life was cursed or destined for a violent end. But by faith, Ashley escaped both physical abduction at gunpoint and emotional abduction by the storms of her life. With Nichols' permission, she walked to freedom. When the police surrounded her apartment, Nichols gave himself up without a fight.

Like Ashley, you may feel that you are trapped. Your captivity may be a financial problem, a life-threatening sickness, marital problems, a persecuting boss or any number of circumstances—even the glass ceiling of unfulfilled dreams. There are indeed things we long to accomplish that seem just outside our grasp. We can see them, yet we keep bumping our heads on invisible barriers. Unfulfilled dreams can be a painful part of our emotional battlefield.

Whatever your struggle, Ashley Smith is a wonderful example of what can happen when you turn your crisis into a ministry moment—when you keep your head in the game. Drawing on the fruit of the Spirit (see Galatians 5:22), she saved two people's lives—hers and her abductor's—and responded in a manner beyond the normal person's emotional range. At the end of the ordeal, she convinced Brian Nichols to go out in a blaze of glory—not with gunshots and anger, but with humility and strength.

Thus, Ashley Smith became a heroine. She reminds me of Abigail from the Old Testament, who bravely placed herself in danger to avert the bloodshed looming between King David and her husband, Nabal. Like Ashley, Abigail approached David and his men with wisdom and with a servant's heart. And, like Ashley, she was able to defuse a potentially violent confrontation.

Heroism, you see, does not have gender. In fact, all through the ages, there have been women who became warriors. Noted archaeologists Mona Behan and Jeannine Davis-Kimball wrote a compelling book entitled *Warrior Women: An Archaeologist's Search for History's Hidden Heroines*. The back cover reads: "*Warrior Women* . . . is the first portrait of women who daringly built civilizations, repelled invaders, and helped to conquer new worlds."

If women have been great warriors in the secular realm, then what greater deeds can Christian women accomplish in the spiritual war that honors Christ? The magnificence of Christianity is that every person has a unique calling. Every individual counts in God's economy. Every person has a piece of God's plan to transform our world. Secretly, we all know that we have been created for a specific assignment. Even people who have never met Christ believe there is a reason they were born.

Many Christians search their entire lives for a chance at greatness because they misunderstand the dynamics of Christ's Kingdom. At first, you may dream of becoming the next Bill Gates or president of the United States. Eventually, you settle on more realistic goals. Perhaps it is to become involved in a political campaign, to join a church, to set money aside for your retirement or for your children's education. Whatever the goal, it is important for you to define your life goals and embrace a sense of purpose.

Perhaps you have found guidance in this regard through books like *The Purpose-Driven Life* or other materials that have helped you understand the broad, foundational "highway" you are traveling, the meaning of your existence.

But what about the specific role God has given you, your home address, so to speak, on that broad highway of humanity? *The Way of the Warrior* will help you identify your own house, your own destiny. Finding and fulfilling one's personal destiny is every person's highest goal. This book is designed as a training manual that will give you a step-by-step approach to becoming a person of influence on your "block," the sphere of your God-given calling. *The Way of the Warrior* will prepare you to enter a zone of maximum impact by changing how you view and respond to the world around you.

Although this book will draw on the entire Bible, you will be encouraged to examine your life and opportunities through two scriptural lenses. The first lens is the life of David, one of God's greatest warriors. His life will be the primary scriptural illustration of the principles described.

The second lens is a strategic framework represented by an acrostic that spells out the word *WARRIOR*. You cannot play basketball without hoops or football without goal lines. In a similar way, trying to understand the subject of spiritual warfare without the strategic Kingdom objectives that guide its purpose is at best fruitless and at worst the domain of thrill-seekers or those interested only in survival. The *WARRIOR* acrostic sets 21st-century goals, while grappling with 21st-century issues. Its seven teachings are based on the following topics:

Wealth (using your influence effectively)

Achievement (melding success and destiny in the Kingdom)

Righteousness (representing God's heart and character)

Reflection (thinking like Jesus)

Intercession (learning active and listening prayer)

Outlook (choosing attitudes and beatitudes)

Reconciliation (building bridges of healed relationships)

Each one of these areas will be addressed in chapters 3 through 9, based upon David's life and times. Using him as a springboard, we will discuss these weighty issues in a practical, hands-on way. Each chapter will include an inspiring account of a contemporary "warrior's life" and a call to action.

Another way to understand the goal of this book is to think about the way professional athletes develop. Most professional athletes start out as kids with a knack for sports. After discovering this natural talent, they invest time and energy in developing themselves. This development may take the form of strength training, running or nutrition. A broad athletic foundation is often laid in the lives of these future Hall of Famers and superstars. Eventually they choose the game they are most suited for. Then, they master their signature sport and find their place in it.

Shaquille O'Neal is an excellent example of this principle. He was very tall in grade school. Blessed with size and strength, he could play any sport. His raw skill could have given him professional stature in a range of athletic endeavors. But, despite his obvious ability, it took him a long time to choose his primary sport. During a rare television interview, Shaq's mother said that he loved football but abandoned it because competitors always aimed at his legs. Injuries clearly would lay ahead if he continued to play. Basketball, on the other hand, allowed him to use his athletic prowess with less danger of career-ending injuries. With basketball, he was able to reach his full potential as an athlete. The rest, as they say, is history.

Let me compare Shaq's experience to our development in Christ. Like Shaq, we often try many different things before we land on the specific calling that the Lord has for us. If we are wise enough to develop our spirituality, character and unique giftings, we will eventually touch an area of greatness and fulfillment.

It is important to remember that great teams are not just the result of individual superstars. In Christ's Kingdom there are often thousands of supporting players for every public "superstar" Christian. First Corinthians 12 helps us understand that the less beautiful parts of the body are actually more honored by God than the seemingly most gifted parts of the team. Paul goes on to inform the Ephesian church that when people work together over a long period of time, it creates an opportunity for exchange and growth. When they do so with an attitude of love, it also releases a corporate witness for Christ in the world (see Ephesians 4:16).

None of the time that we spend developing this core spirituality and grace in our lives is wasted. God has pre-wired us with natural talents and loaded us with brilliant software called "gifts of the Spirit." The process of coordinating our natural and spiritual gifts is similar to Shaq's development in agility and strength.

He always knew that he would be a great competitor. It was only a matter of time before he found the game he was best suited for.

The Way of the Warrior will help develop the spiritual person within you. Applying the principles of this book will give you a new spiritual bearing and aptitude that will allow you to make a clear contribution for Christ in the world.

The Reality of War

Men are often fascinated by war. Just look at the popularity of the action-movie genre. Hollywood plays on this natural interest by producing films that are nothing more than shooting, bombing, exploding, kickboxing fests. They glorify violence, failing to depict its true horror, and have desensitized an entire generation to bloody mayhem.

Movies also have created what I call the "cult of the false hero." In these settings, the hero never dies. He gets the girl, loses the girl and finally reconnects with the girl. He rises to conquer no matter how many times he gets shot. No wonder the Columbine or Red Lake killers committed mass murder with such ease! They were living in the Twilight Zone world of the "cult of the false hero." The real-life devastation that these mass murders caused was staggering.

Hollywood aside, war is actually one of the least attractive subjects to write about. As I prayed about writing this book, I realized that many Christians do not understand the stark reality of their experiences on earth. Life is not a phantom flickering on a movie screen; winning or losing at spiritual warfare has eternal results. The moment a person is born again, he or she becomes identified with a King and a Kingdom.

The enemy's forces align against us, personally. The war with Iraq has made us familiar with the high price of military conflict. Death is always a part of the equation, sometimes in grotesque ways. Terrorists in the Middle East are delighted to behead helpless captives, for example, because of the shock such acts create. Add a dash of television coverage and the intended effect is magnified. As an ancient Chinese proverb states, "Kill one, teach a thousand."

Christians must be aware that our spiritual enemies are just as devious and ruthless as our natural enemies. They rejoice at the spiritual death of spiritual brothers through apostasy. Yet they are perhaps even happier when a pastor falls into sexual sin with one of his parishioners or when an angry Christian discredits Christ through narrow-mindedness or bigotry. The enemies of our souls sing gleefully when they can point out gross hypocrisy in the lives of the people of God. Once our comrades fall, all too often other Christians finish them off with accusation, rejection or gossip.

Let me emphasize this: Our battle is not something that we can experience vicariously with popcorn and sodas in hand. We are involved in a real war with a real enemy. Training and discipline are crucial for our survival.

The Discipline of Warfare

Spiritual war, like natural war, is waged with strategic goals on many fronts. Control of the skies, for example, is essential in modern warfare. As Christians think about air control, we could equate this critical dimension of war to the power of prayer. Although Satan is the prince of the power of the air (see Ephesians 2:2), we can defeat his forces with focused, persistent prayer.

Our land strategies, on the other hand, have to include occupying or transforming critical posts in politics and law, plus positions in the arts, entertainment, fashion, sports, education, business and the organized Church. Each of these arenas is an important site that must be protected. The rampant pedophilia cases plaguing the Roman Catholic Church have brought reproach upon the entire Christian Church and serve as a warning of what happens when our guard is lowered. The media, of course, have sensationalized this deplorable situation to the point that it has weakened the confidence many Catholics have in their church. Unfortunately, these sins are not limited to one part of the Body; informed people believe that it is only a matter of time before similar sexual improprieties are exposed in the evangelical Church.

In light of this, the Church's ground battle must focus on raising up leaders who cannot be tempted to misuse their authority. Jesus said of Himself, "The prince of this world cometh, and hath nothing in me" (John 14:30, KJV). Those in positions of significant spiritual authority must live above reproach so that, like Jesus, the enemy has nothing in them—and nothing on them, either. There is a little-quoted passage in the New Testament that expresses the way spiritual guardians of high posts should think of themselves:

> "For there are some eunuchs, which were so born from their mother's womb: and there are some eunuchs, which were made eunuchs of men: and there be eunuchs, which have made themselves eunuchs for the kingdom of heaven's sake. He that is able to receive it, let him receive it."
>
> Matthew 19:12, KJV

Christian leaders must be so dead to temptation in their areas of responsibility that they are like eunuchs of old employed by kings to guard the women in their harems.

To prevent further damage to Christianity at large, ministers must be trained theologically, tested in character and moral fidelity and examined psychologically more intensely than ever before.

These same kinds of safeguards must also be created for those with a mission to the film industry or politics or any other visible field. Victory in these areas can be won only by spiritual soldiers who cannot be bought or sold. Discipleship from the early teenage years must be part of the master plan. Specialized support groups and mentoring are also indispensable components.

Becoming a world-class warrior demands a lifestyle based upon discipline, commitment and the Word of God. What if there was a Christian version of the Navy Seals? Would you want to enlist? There is such a group! The only requirements are a true love for Jesus and a willing heart. That is all you have to bring. Everything else can be learned.

Unfortunately, we cannot just jump into an elite fighting force. If you sought a career in the U.S. military, it would make sense to talk to someone who has "been there." Take Colin Powell, for instance. How much learning time would you save if you could phone him anytime you had a question? Access to coaching assistance from champions could certainly help you keep your head in the game.

As I have noted, your coach in this book is going to be David, one of the greatest warriors of all time. We will learn directly from his writings and those of his son Solomon (renowned for his wisdom). What set David apart from many in history was his ability to use his spiritual skills along with his natural skills. He discerned

God's guidance, used God's principles and rose from obscurity to national prominence overnight. As you read this book, I hope it will be like listening to David discuss the finer points of walking with God through some of the greatest adventures of all time. In addition, I hope to give you insights on how to translate that knowledge into action.

Over the years, I have studied various war traditions and have learned that warriors, like athletes, must develop certain core skills. Call these skills "basic training." Basic training must be finished before we go on to specialized areas of service or advanced training. The next chapter will give you the first step in this basic training; after that we will hear directly from David. In the next chapter we will examine how to think about "the war" from a biblical perspective and how you can develop your core strengths as a warrior. But first, let us take an inventory of what we have learned so far and how it applies to your life.

TAKING INVENTORY

Analyze the war zones in your life by answering each of these questions.

1. What is my primary struggle?
   a. Ashley Smith was abducted and held hostage. I have been:
   b. This is how I feel about my situation:
   c. Here are some positive things I can do about my situation:
2. Is there a secondary front in my battle?
   a. My job is difficult because:
   b. My family is troubled because:
   c. Other significant challenges include:

2

Warriors and Warfare

Fight the Right War in the Right Way

The soldier's trade, if it is to mean anything at all, has to be anchored to an unshakeable code of honor. Otherwise, those of us who follow the drums become nothing more than a bunch of hired assassins walking around in gaudy clothes , , , a disgrace to God and mankind.

Prussian Major General Carl von Clausewitz

T. D. Jakes' critique was inspired. I had just given an interview on Christian television about an emerging shift in the political views of black churchgoers, when the nationally known preacher took me aside. "Your message should be on secular TV," he said. "This is the wrong place for this information." This was only one month before the presidential election in 2004.

With seasoned insight, Jakes suggested a course of action, concluding pensively that I had only a brief "window of opportunity" for my message—until election day. Inwardly, the light went on. I knew he was right, and I had the sense that he was speaking more than just man's wisdom; he was speaking the Lord's guiding word to me.

Like an ex-fighter-turned-coach who had been in the ring in every kind of situation, Jakes had a sense of the game. In every fight movie there is a trainer in the ring who whispers in the ear of the boxer. For a moment, the famed T. D. Jakes joined the world's greatest "boxing" coaches. My challenge that night was to let no one else do my work for me. And there was also no guarantee that I would be successful in getting my message heard. But I learned a powerful lesson that night: Real champions translate instructions into creative action. They turn workouts into victories, dreams into reality. No matter how great the trainer, the fighter still has to win for himself.

Subsequent events have confirmed that T. D. Jakes spoke to me as a voice from God. None of the amazing things that occurred could have happened, I believe, without the Lord's mighty hand at work. It was certainly nothing I could have accomplished on my own, or even considered. That is something I want to stress.

Deciding to obey what I believed was the Lord's word, I found what followed breathtaking. Within a month, an article I wrote appeared on the front page of the New York *Sun Times*. Other pieces quickly appeared in newspapers in Washington, Chicago and other cities around the nation. Interviewers began lining up. I was asked to do more than thirty interviews in less than a month. CBS's *Evening News* followed me around for a couple of days, and Bill O'Reilly interviewed me on his nightly program.

Within six months, 104 newspapers, magazines and radio and television stations had sought me out to hear my message about the shifting political voice of black voters. At one point, I found myself sitting on the same stage with Jesse Jackson, Cornel West, Joseph Lowery, Minister Farrakhan and a handful of the nation's secular black leaders. Although my conservative biblical views were different from theirs, I was excited that the message the Lord had charged me to give was broadcast to more than one hundred million people.

As I look back on those months of extreme acceleration, I have no doubt that my conversation with T. D. Jakes in that television station's waiting room, the "green room," as it is called, was a divine encounter. God sent a credible man as a road sign on life's highway, a sign that read: "Change Lanes and Speed Up."

Understand that I could have resisted the Lord's guidance. I have, at times. We all have. Growing in wisdom is always a choice. Understand, too, that I took specific steps of faith in response to the gift of godly counsel. Faith must be mixed with action. Without action, a word can die and a season can pass. If I had been hardhearted, preoccupied with the world's cares and pleasures or otherwise deaf to the Lord's guidance—or unwilling to act—He would have found someone else to give His message. I am sure of that.

There is something else that is important to understand. There is no such thing as overnight success. Sustainable advances are based upon preparation. So let's look at the basic training we need for fighting the right war in the right way.

The Path

Several years ago, I trained for a marathon. Every Saturday a group of those training met at a beautiful running trail not far from the University of Maryland for our weekly long run. The asphalt path was tree lined, making it cool in the summer. Visibility, however, was limited. You could see only a few hundred yards ahead at a time. Sometimes we would go around a corner and the terrain would totally change. The challenge was that all of us were non-runners. We had agreed to raise money for HIV-AIDS research. Although a marathon seemed daunting to this former football player, a dear friend of mine coaxed me into what he called a "spiritual" experience.

Each week we ran farther than I had ever run in my life. Week after grueling week it went. We eventually finished a 26.2-mile practice run one month before the actual event.

I learned three things from my long distance training. In preparing for each Saturday's run, I would first look inward, repeating to myself, *You can make it today*. Second, I would look upward in prayer to draw strength from God. Finally, I would look outward at the path. Braced emotionally and encouraged spiritually, I was able to deal with the difficulties of a ten- or fifteen-mile weekend run. Let's look a little more closely at these stages of preparation.

Looking In

To say that the warrior in basic training must look inside may sound confusing. Perhaps even a little New Age or metaphysical. Nothing could be farther from the truth. Self-examination is fundamental to Christianity. Paul states clearly that by judging yourself, you can avoid external chastening from God (see 1 Corinthians 11:32–34). Looking inside is the first step. Staying on course with God is the essence of what the Scriptures call righteousness.

Proverbs 4:18 says, "The path of the righteous is like the first gleam of dawn, shining ever brighter till the full light of day." Solomon's words here describe the life journey of his father, David. David was never perfect. In fact, he committed many sins. Yet he had a habit of always repenting, even if it took a little time. His willingness to repent and get back into relationship with God made him different from King Saul, for example. David grew in wisdom and understanding and learned the power of righteousness in his life, and God blessed him abundantly.

Psalm 37:23–25 shows that the inner attitude of righteousness is essential for personal success:

> If the LORD delights in a man's way, he makes his steps firm; though he stumble, he will not fall, for the LORD upholds him with his hand. I was young and now I am old, yet I have never seen the righteous forsaken or their children begging bread.

For years, I have delighted in knowing that the longer I walk with Christ, as a committed believer, the clearer my path will become. If you meet the requirements, you do not have to worry about unexpected curves in the road. On the other hand, going your own way in disobedience, walking apart from God, produces the opposite result. Proverbs 4:19 says, "The way of the wicked is like deep darkness; they do not know what makes them stumble."

The Scriptures promise you purpose, prosperity and peace if you walk in God's ways. This is the path of personal victory, eternal impact and spiritual success. The question each of us faces is whether or not we are willing to pay the price to walk the path of the warrior. Too many of us are doing our own thing. We want God to bless our mess or rearrange our mistakes. We must realize that we are the salt of the earth and the light of the world (see Matthew 5:13–14). Having a proper spiritual focus will not only help us solve our personal problems but also help us become lifelines to others.

Looking Up

The ancient Israelites had a tradition of singing select psalms as they made pilgrimages to Jerusalem three times a year. Fifteen psalms were used in this process. These psalms, or songs, helped the pilgrims focus on the Lord and prepared them to meet with God on the high holy days.

One of my favorite "songs of ascent," as they are called, is Psalm 121. The first three verses are especially poignant:

> I lift up my eyes to the hills—where does my help come from? My help comes from the LORD, the Maker of heaven and earth. He will not let your foot slip—he who watches over you will not slumber.

"Lifting up our eyes" is a way of saying we seek God's guidance as we look toward our destination. Wellington Boone, best known for his Promise Keepers messages and ministry, puts it this way: "Pray there before you go there." Powerful advances into God's purposes are often preceded by powerful prayer. Praise and worship are also effective tools of intercession. The Scriptures suggest that praise stops the advance of our enemies in the spiritual realm (see Psalm 8:2). Those of us called to be warriors must learn to worship as we move forward on our paths of purpose.

Looking Out

Like embarking on a long distance run, we will go farther than ever before when we remember to look in, look up and look out. Only after we have prayed about our motives and desires (looking in) and prayed about our destination (looking up) can we really be ready to seize the wonderful opportunities before us (looking out). Moments like this happen only for those already on a path. Jesus said you cannot see the Kingdom of God unless you are born again. Ironically, words of wisdom are whirring past us all the time. Desperation alone does not always yield insight. Our eyes must truly be open. Success in spiritual war is impossible without wisdom. Solomon said that wisdom is literally calling to us from the streets (see Proverbs 8:1–4). So how do we position ourselves to hear all this wisdom?

None of us can predict when battles will occur. We can, however, train and prepare and learn which battles we should fight. The ancient Chinese military strategist Sun Tzu said,

> If you know the enemy and know yourself, you need not fear the result of a hundred battles. If you know yourself but not the enemy, for every victory gained you will also suffer a defeat. If you know neither the enemy nor yourself, you will succumb in every battle.[1]

The three steps we have just explored—look in, look up, look out—mesh nicely with his advice to know ourselves and our resources. As we walk or jog down a new path, God will teach us much about our enemy. But our lives should not focus on the darkness: We are walking toward the light.

People of the Way

In titling this book *The Way of the Warrior*, I am referring to more than just the approach or lifestyle of the soldier engaged in spiritual warfare. The words *the way* are full of significance. Jesus described both Himself (see John 14:6–7) and the true spiritual walk as the Way. Matthew 7:14 says, "Small is the gate and narrow the road that leads to life, and only a few find it." This imagery is repeated over and over again in the Scriptures.

The *New Bible Dictionary* explains that "'the Way' was the oldest designation of the Christian church for itself." God's people have historically viewed themselves as individuals with different starting points along a common path. The issue is not where we start; the depth of our sin before salvation does not condemn us. The real issue is whether or not we are willing to be led along God's way. The earliest description of the followers of Christ was, therefore, "people of the Way."

Paul spoke repeatedly of "the Way." Talking to people familiar with the Jewish faith, for instance, he said, "I admit that I worship the God of our fathers as a follower of the Way"(Acts 24:14). The book of Acts describes how the citizens of Ephesus viewed him: "Paul entered the synagogue and spoke boldly there for three months, arguing persuasively about the kingdom of God. But some of them became obstinate; they refused to believe and publicly maligned the Way" (Acts 19:8–9). Acts 19:23 states: "About that time there arose a great disturbance about the Way." In Acts 24:22 we read that even Felix, the Roman governor, was well acquainted with the Way.

The Way of the Warrior is a code of honor. It is a metaphor for a high-impact life, lived without compromise.

Borrowing from an Eastern Concept

The Christian walk is designed to produce personal victory, a life of "joy unspeakable and full of glory" (1 Peter 1:8, KJV). Yet, despite our position in Christ, many of us reach only a small portion of our potential. Jesus described levels of productivity in Matthew 13, Mark 4 and Luke 8. There seem to be 30, 60 and 100 percent Christians. The warrior's code obviously aims at producing 100 percent fruitful believers. One hundred percent fruitfulness will allow us to influence the culture with our enthusiasm and faith.

As we think about developing a uniquely Christian code of honor, let's begin by observing one of the world's approaches to training real soldiers. Let me note that it is not unscriptural to use information from different cultures if it advances our purposes. The apostle Paul gave us a principle for learning spiritual concepts from natural life. He said, "The spiritual did not come first, but the natural, and after that the spiritual" (1 Corinthians 15:46).

Within the samurai culture in Japan there existed a philosophy called *bushido*. This was known as "The Way of the Warrior." The teaching continued into the days of World War II when followers of the code became kamikaze pilots, willing to sacrifice their lives by flying their planes into American battleships. They were willing to die for what they believed; it is a tragic commentary that most Christians cannot even *live* the things they hold dear.

When someone became a samurai, he was agreeing to die at the behest of his earthly lord. In fact, he began his service with the idea that he was already dead. Does this sound like the Christian walk? When we start on the path of salvation, we must be willing to die at the behest of God. In other words, when you became a Christian you gave up your rights, your privileges. As Jesus' servant, you are called to give your life to Christ.

Once this is settled in your heart, you will not resist when God asks you to do something. Yet, many of us get into a quandary and start "seeking God" more about things that rub against our flesh. If we have pledged to give our lives, then what is the problem when He asks us to give a little bit of money, go on a fast or whatever? We begin to question whether or not we can handle that kind of commitment. The problem is that we did not understand what we were called to at the beginning—to lay down our lives and enter a war zone.

You cannot be a "commando" Christian unless you understand that your death has already been required by your commitment to the cross. Baptism is a covenant act in which we say to Christ, "We are dead to the world, but alive in you" (see Colossians 2:12). Understand that I am not advocating physical war here. I am looking at the core tenets of a classic warrior tradition.

For samurai, a code of conduct preceded training in weaponry techniques and combat maneuvers. In a similar way, Christians must be firm on the path to Christian maturity before we learn the techniques of conquest. The samurai code consists of the following seven principles:

Gi: rectitude or principled decision making
Yu: courage
Jin: benevolence
Rei: respect
Makoto: honesty
Meiyo: honor
Chugi: loyalty

The code of the samurai is quite a challenge—though each one of the principles has a biblical corollary. But this is where we part with the world's teaching: Jesus did not call us to be samurai; He called us to be Christians. Yet, if we cannot do at least what the samurai did, we are not fit for much. The code above has to be carried out in the strength of the flesh. How much more can we be empowered to live for Christ in a higher, more dynamic way?

The Lord is looking for revolutionary men and women, followers willing to set high standards for themselves. Perhaps we should think of ourselves as modern-day knights and ladies who live to carry out the wishes of the king. Erwin McManus, author of the book *Uprising* and senior leader of the Mosaic Church, said it this way: "There is a place where few of us aspire to, where the measure of our worth is not how much we have, but how much we give of ourselves."[2] In the next chapter, we will look at the first of seven principles in the way of the Christian warrior. But, before we do that, let's take another inventory of what we have learned.

TAKING INVENTORY

1. What are my key goals?
   a. What is my most important goal in my career?
   b. What is my most important goal for my family?
   c. What is my most important goal in my church?
   d. What is my most important goal in my hobby or recreation?
   e. What goals do I have in my community or for public service?
2. Am I willing to "look in" and take a personal inventory?
   a. Which of my friendships are questionable?

   b. Which friendships strengthen my walk with God?
   c. What reading materials would help me?
3. Am I willing to "look up" and draw strength? Which
   spiritual disciplines do I need to strengthen?
   • Prayer?
   • Bible reading?
   • Fasting?
   • Giving?
   • Evangelism?
   • Worship?
4. Am I willing to "look out"?
   a. Are there things about my future that make me
      anxious?
   b. How would I define nobility for myself?

3

Wealth and Influence

God's Power Brokers

The best leaders understand that leadership is the liberation of talent; hence they gain power not only by constantly giving it away, but also by not grabbing it back.

Major-General Perry M. Smith

Florence Nightingale came to fame in 19th-century Europe as an angel of mercy and intelligence during the horrors of the Crimean War. A million lives were lost in this war against Russian dominance.

It began when an ambitious Russian tsar came to power. The age-old dream of world conquest loomed heavily in the vision of the Russian military. Turkey declared war on aggressive Russia in late 1853 and was joined a few months later by Great Britain and France's own declaration of war against the tsar. The "modern" weapons of the day meant extreme numbers of casualties. During the height of the war, the Russians alone were losing a thousand men a day. The British army lost more than fourteen thousand men, despite superior weaponry and a huge allied military force.

Ironically, though, more men were dying in makeshift hospitals because of disease than were being killed on the battlefield. To make things worse, there were no trained nurses. In those days the women who helped on the front were seen as less than honorable. In fact, many people assumed that these women were prostitutes or alcoholics. Florence came into this mêlée at the age of 34. By the end of the war in 1856, she had revolutionized the field of nursing. Living to the ripe old age of ninety, Nightingale became a major champion of education for women in both Britain and the U.S.

Perhaps the most impressive thing about this amazing woman was the connection she made with everyday people. The chorus of a popular song written and sung during the Crimean war went like this:

> Her heart it means good for no bounty she'll take,
> She'd lay down her life for the poor soldier's sake.
> She prays for the dying, she gives peace to the brave,
> She feels that the soldier has a soul to be saved.
> The wounded they love her as it has been seen,
> She's the soldier's preserver, they call her their queen.
> May God give her strength, and her heart never fail,
> One of heaven's best gifts is Miss Nightingale.[1]

There is no question that this woman was one of God's choice warriors. In addition to her medical work in the Crimean War, Florence organized record-keeping procedures and cleaned up the hospitals. Brilliant in mathematics, Florence revolutionized mathematical analysis of social phenomena. She created a "polar-area diagram" in order to dramatize the needless deaths caused by unsanitary conditions.

Florence's statistical analysis and her consequent sanitary reform lowered the mortality rate significantly. The improvements she made in medical and surgical procedures were revolutionary and became forerunners for our contemporary practices. Her abilities in statistics and their analysis led to her becoming a Fellow of the Royal Statistical Society and an honorary member of the American Statistical Association. Florence was called a "prophetess" in the advancement of applied statistics.

So where did this young woman come from? How did she get the courage to stand up and change the entire nation's approach to medicine? First of all, she came from a devout family that passed on their faith. Her grandfather was a member of the House of Lords in England. Going beyond any tradition of the day, her father, William, decided that this little girl and her sister would not miss out on any of the academic preparation that young gentlemen received. Along with special tutoring in the sciences, she learned five languages, including Greek; her father was known to read devotional passages to her from the New Testament in the original Greek. Perhaps most notable, she was taught how to use the gifts of wealth and influence that she had inherited.

When Nightingale was seventeen years old, she had a visitation from the Lord. Some writers describe it as an angelic visitation in which she was told that the Lord had placed a special calling upon her life. It was several years before she understood that calling. After spending a year as the volunteer head of an institution for "gentlewomen in illness," the British secretary of war called upon her and 38 other women to serve in the Crimean War.

Florence embodied the first Davidic model for warriors that we will study: the use of wealth and influence to fulfill the call of God upon our lives. First of all, she did not let others define her. Second, she combined heart and head to change her world. Third, she was not tempted by materialism. Fourth, she kept growing and set a high standard of excellence. Finally, she fought for those who could not fight for themselves.

The rest of the chapter will more fully describe David's model of wealth and influence, also describing the "Ten Commandments of Influence" he handed down to Solomon. These commandments prepare the warrior to "think the right way" about both finance and influence.

David's Game Plan

This chapter is not specifically about how to make money. It is about how to position yourself to be in authority so that as you control money, you garner influence. People who understand how to negotiate the terrain of power can change their worlds. John F. Kennedy said it this way: "Wealth is the means, and people are the ends. All our material riches will avail us little if we do not use them to expand the opportunities of our people."[2]

This is a time when many Christians have become enamored of the prayer of Jabez to the point of missing opportunities of community service and ministry for fear of doing harm. For many of us, advancing in this arena will require us to change our thinking radically. Breaking the kind of thinking patterns that lead us to self-sabotage and fear of achievement is a vital step to becoming a great warrior for God.

Similar to Florence Nightingale, David heard about his calling before he understood how God would bring it into reality. During Samuel's prophetic visit to his home, David was anointed as God's choice for king even though Saul still sat on the throne. How would such a destiny be fulfilled?

It began one day with a surprise summons for David to go serve the king: David knew that it was God's invitation, as we will see in a moment. The Scripture below tells the story:

> So Saul said to his attendants, "Find someone who plays [the harp] well and bring him to me." One of the servants answered, "I have seen a son of Jesse of Bethlehem who knows how to play the harp. He is a brave man and a warrior. He speaks well and is a fine-looking man. And the LORD is with him."
>
> 1 Samuel 16:17–18

What are the chances that the king would call an unknown shepherd boy to come work in his court? When David first heard the prophetic word from Samuel that he would become king, I am sure that he was a little confused. Even if he had an inward sense of a great calling, there seemed to be no bridge to take him there. But the Lord opened the way for him through his natural gift of worship; the king needed a harpist and David was ready. No wonder Solomon wrote by observation: "A man's gift makes room for him and brings him before great men" (Proverbs 18:16, NASB).

David knew that this was the Lord's invitation because the first step in his game plan had been to develop his natural gifts for the Lord to use. Because he did not squander his talents, he saw his destiny begin to unfold.

The second step was to grow secretly in his calling to be king. Once David was in Saul's house, he could not announce to everyone that he was there to take over. The truth is that much of what he was there to learn was on the "Don't Do This" list. At this stage of life, Saul, who had reigned for many years, was at a spiritual nadir. David committed many moral sins in the years to follow, but he did not repeat the same sins as Saul.

The application of this principle for us is that we must not despise the days of small beginnings. Sometimes on-the-job training is the most important thing God can give us. A modern example of this is the story of Joel Osteen of Lakewood Church in Houston. Unlike David, Joel was not sent to serve a sinful leader. Quite the contrary. He dropped out of a prestigious Christian university to return home and serve in his godly father's ministry. For years, he simply sought to make his father's television program the best it could possibly be. Often asked to speak, he never accepted the opportunity until the Sunday before his father died. Unknown to the young Osteen, he was in training to become one of America's most prominent ministers. God has a plan for each of us, and faithful service is always a prerequisite to enter into His plan.

The third step in David's game plan was to wait patiently for God to orchestrate his personal promotion. That step into the limelight led him into the shadow of a giant: Goliath. I think that David had a feeling that Goliath's challenge to his nation was his moment of moving into prominence. It was the right moment, and he grasped it.

It is important to note that if this had not been the right time, if he had acted hastily in pursuit of his dream, he could have lost the unique position of influence he was developing during his early days in the court. David was on staff with the king, but at the time of Goliath's challenge, he was obviously at home. He was doing the day-to-day stuff of life—taking care of the sheep, living in God's presence outside of public scrutiny. While delivering supplies to his brothers on one occasion, David learned of the giant's taunts against Israel. The Scripture below shows that David was evaluating this opportunity for its promotional aspects:

> David asked the men standing near him, "What will be done for the man who kills this Philistine and removes this disgrace from Israel? Who is this uncircumcised Philistine that he should defy the armies of the living God?" They repeated to him what they had been saying and told him, "This is what will be done for the man who kills him."
>
> 1 Samuel 17:26–27

And finally, as David grew older in years, in the culmination of his destiny, he understood that the wealth he acquired over a lifetime was to be used by others for the work of God. We may find that some things we desire to promote and build up are not actually part of our personal callings. We may have been raised up to give the next generation a head start. The passage below shows David's realization of this fact of generational life:

> King David rose to his feet and said: "Listen to me, my brothers and my people. I had it in my heart to build a house as a place of rest for the ark of the covenant of the LORD, for the footstool of our God and I made plans to build it. But God said to me, 'You are not to build a house for my Name, because you are a warrior and have shed blood.'"
>
> 1 Chronicles 28:2–3

In David's case, the prohibition against his building a house for God seems to have been more of a punishment than a basic generational distinction. David's sin with Bathsheba and his murder of her husband may well have reaped this punishment. Like Moses striking the rock, David's actions may have so misrepresented the heart and character of God that He could not let this leader have the assignment of a lifetime.

Even so, despite this disappointment, David opened the treasury of the kingdom and his personal wealth to promote God's work through Solomon. His fortunes were not amassed for selfish desires.

> Then King David said to the whole assembly: "My son Solomon, the one whom God has chosen, is young and inexperienced. The task is great, because this palatial structure is not for man but for the LORD God. With all my resources I have provided for the temple of my God—gold for the gold work, silver for the silver, bronze for the bronze, iron for the iron and wood for the wood, as well as onyx for the settings, turquoise, stones of various colors, and all kinds of fine stone and marble—all of these in large quantities. Besides, in my devotion to the temple of my God I now give my personal treasures of gold and silver for the temple of my God, over and above everything I have provided for this holy temple."
>
> 1 Chronicles 29:1–3

The Ten Commandments of Influence

Now that we understand the game plan that David demonstrated for physical prosperity and influence, we will focus more on how we qualify to receive this blessing of wealth. In the Hebrew mindset, prosperity always followed lifelong obedience. Proverbs 10:22 summarizes the concept well: "The blessing of the LORD brings wealth, and he adds no trouble to it."

As already stated, Solomon's teachings will be used to enunciate both his and David's family concept of how to attain wealth the right way. The New Testament is clear that seeking wealth for wealth's sake is an exercise in folly. Heed Solomon's words, therefore, realizing that consumption for consumption's sake can be destructive. These Ten Commandments of Influence are garnered from Proverbs 22:1–23.

1. Release the Twin Sisters of Blessing

"A good name is more desirable than great riches; to be esteemed is better than silver or gold" (Proverbs 22:1).

The twin sisters of blessing are *A Good Name* and *Favor*. Faithfulness is essential in creating a good name. Take credit ratings. If a person has paid his bills on time and kept his word financially, he will have a good credit rating. Whether we realize it or not, we are also developing a "relational" credit rating as we interact with people in both business and recreation. If that rating is high, we will get the "benefit of the doubt." People will assume the best of us, even in questionable situations. A good name is very important.

I have chosen *Favor* as the twin sister of *A Good Name* because God's favor is often essential to set up the opportunity to develop a good name. Favor is sometimes like a spotlight that allows us to be recognized by others. Favor may cause people to believe in our potential or respect our opinions. Favor can get us in the door, but faithfulness will keep us there. Favor may cause people to reach out to us, but faithfulness will allow a deep relationship to develop.

Several years ago, for example, our church's real estate brokers recommended we investigate an 87-acre property just outside the eastern part of the city. Many church leaders had talked to the owner about purchasing the site. From the first day the owner and I met, there seemed to be a special chemistry between us. By the time our church purchased the property, the owner gave our ministry more than $200,000 in cash along with equipment and furnishings valued at more than $100,000. During the years we have known this gentleman, we have had an opportunity to share the Gospel with him. Naturally, we have sought to maintain a faithful relationship with this generous man.

2. Pursue Operational Wisdom

"Rich and poor have this in common: The LORD is the Maker of them all. A prudent man sees danger and takes refuge, but the simple keep going and suffer for it" (Proverbs 22:2–3).

I was thirteen when I got my first job. I started out stuffing envelopes, processing a thousand pieces of mail all by myself. I know there is equipment for that kind of work, but I learned how to do this on purpose so that when the power went out, my skill took over. If we don't learn how to do *something*, we will know how to do *nothing* when modern conveniences fail. If Donald Trump were put out on the street today without any cash, would he know how to start over and get money? He sure would! This is because he has operational wisdom; he knows how to make money.

"A prudent man sees danger and takes refuge, but the simple keep going and suffer for it." We need to be able to discern the seasons when God is moving. The guiding question of operational wisdom is, "What does this kind of wisdom look like?" We need to know what it looks like so that when we are looking at it, we can identify it.

And in the meantime we must prepare. Jesus told His disciples, "I am telling you this now, so that when it comes to pass you will know what you are looking at" (see John 13:19). We need to develop skill and work at our craft in order to recognize and use operational wisdom. If we do not prepare, God cannot give us anything. Otherwise, if He gives it to us, we will not know what to do with it.

3. Refine Godly Character

"Humility and the fear of the LORD bring wealth and honor and life. In the paths of the wicked lie thorns and snares, but he who guards his soul stays far from them" (Proverbs 22:4–5).

The secular world would call humility and the fear of the Lord a weakness. God, however, sees these things as His bridle and saddle in our lives. Using the imagery of a well-trained horse, we are of no real good to God's purposes until we can be easily guided by Him. Until a horse is broken of his independence and self-will, it is difficult for him to be used by his master. The inward work of progressive humility unties God's hands concerning finances and influence.

Several years ago I read a book by Dr. Judson Cornwall entitled *Pride.* The book described the problems that pride brings into our lives. As cancer is to our natural bodies, so is pride to our spiritual systems. The more God uses us, the more each of us will be tempted to think that our accomplishments are due to some inherent quality in ourselves. The truth behind our usefulness for God is the mystery of His will. Others could compete with our ability, but God has chosen to use us. When I hear a question like "How did Jackson pull that off?" I know that the Lord uses the foolish things to confound the wise!

This is not to discredit any of us. It is simply to acknowledge that God promotes His agenda, not our charisma or natural skills. He promotes His purpose. No wonder Proverbs 19:21 says, "Many are the plans in a man's heart, but it is the LORD's purpose that prevails."

4. Train a Child

"Train a child in the way he should go, and when he is old he will not turn from it. The rich rule over the poor, and the borrower is servant to the lender. He who sows wickedness reaps trouble, and the rod of his fury will be destroyed. A generous man will himself be blessed, for he shares his food with the poor" (Proverbs 22:6–9).

Robert Kiyosaki wrote a groundbreaking book entitled *Rich Dad, Poor Dad*. This work is designed to pass on a formula for maximizing one's financial status. I mention this because it is never too early to teach—or to learn—biblical principles about finances.

These verses of Scripture tell parents, first, to train their children so that they will live out good principles all their lives. The verses that follow offer three simple points that every young person should understand thoroughly about the influence that comes with wealth:

1. The rich control; the poor are servants.
2. Wickedness will destroy the perpetrator in the long term.
3. Generosity to the poor releases the blessings of God.

The point is not to grow up and get rich. The point is that finances used properly enrich one's service to God.

5. Set the Right Relational Atmosphere

"Drive out the mocker, and out goes strife; quarrels and insults are ended. He who loves a pure heart and whose speech is gracious will have the king for his friend" (Proverbs 22:10–11).

All of us have been in workplaces or service clubs that seem to breed cynicism and negativity. Years ago I thought that everyone wanted to do a good job and to make a difference in the marketplace. This is, unfortunately, not the case. The Bible calls people like this, those who have been so negative for so long, *scorners*. This word in the original Hebrew text implies arrogance and rebellion. These are people who carry a sense of controversy with them everywhere they go. They are the *prima donnas* or drama queens in today's parlance. They don't have peace with God or man.

Sometimes we must remove these individuals from key roles in our lives. The atmosphere will change dramatically when we do. In a business or ministry, it may mean a demotion. In other cases, we may need to stop receiving counsel from them. If you are not in a position of authority over them, you might remove yourself as far as possible from their influence. Once scorners are removed, harmony, blessing and prosperity will rest on your business or organization as part of the Psalm 133 blessing:

> How good and pleasant it is when brothers live together in unity! It is like precious oil poured on the head, running down on the beard, running down on Aaron's beard, down upon the collar of his robes. It is as if the dew of Hermon were falling on Mount Zion. For there the LORD bestows his blessing, even life forevermore.
>
> verses 1–3

Psalm 133 people are diametrically opposed to the scorners. Scorners release controversy wherever they go. Psalm 133 people, conversely, release blessings and grace wherever they go. Proverbs 22:11 points out the fact that there are people who work at promoting unity. These people create an atmosphere of blessing. If we nurture a good attitude and remain open we will, in turn, attract high-level people. These important people need true friends. They want friends who will not manipulate them or seek personal gain at their expense.

Over the years, I have enjoyed strong relationships with well-known leaders around the nation and the world. I have discovered that if I continue to grow and work on myself, the Lord will give me many strategic relationships. There will be important people that I will be called upon to support, serve and love, just because my heart is right. For myself, I consider these kinds of relationships a great blessing from God.

6. Keep Your Spiritual Ears Open

"Pay attention and listen to the sayings of the wise; apply your heart to what I teach" (Proverbs 22:17).

This "commandment" is so clear and simple, it needs no further clarification. Keep listening to the word of God and wise counselors.

7. Take Care of the Needy

"Do not exploit the poor because they are poor and do not crush the needy in court, for the LORD will take up their case and will plunder those who plunder them" (Proverbs 22:22–23).

This is an admonition for those who want to prosper: Never abuse power over the needy. Powerful people may win in an earthly court by hiring the best lawyers and outspending their opponents, but this Scripture is saying that God will ultimately even the score.

My paternal grandmother was a maid and her brother was a chauffeur. I delight in the opportunity now in my travels to tip limousine drivers and maids in hotels. I believe that God will bless me for using every opportunity to help the working poor in our nation.

8. Use Debt Strategically

"Do not be a man who strikes hands in pledge or puts up security for debts; if you lack the means to pay, your very bed will be snatched from under you" (Proverbs 22:26–27).

This Scripture warns against being a cosigner for other people's debts. If you lack the means to pay the bill, you are being very foolhardy. Unlike some teachers, I believe that there is appropriate use of debt. Many companies, for instance, must use debt to create the economy of scale to start a business. One wise business leader once told me, "If your ideas are not good enough for banks and investors to put money into your project, maybe you shouldn't invest in it either."

The Lord has blessed the way Western businesses have used debt and equity to fund their businesses. Unfortunately, in recent years many businesses have taken on a Scrooge-like quality in their approach to their employees. Others lack financial integrity in their businesses. Integrity and generosity should be at the heart of any approach to business.

9. Maintain Integrity Even When It Hurts

"Do not move an ancient boundary stone set up by your forefathers" (Proverbs 22:28).

Moving boundary lines is a form of stealing. Six times the Bible mentions the sin of moving boundary stones (see Deuteronomy 19:14; 27:17; Job 24:2; Proverbs 22:28; 23:10; Hosea 5:10). This could be a tempting sin for a farmer, who could easily increase the size of his farm by simply moving the stones at the boundary lines. As stated above, the long-term blessings of God follow those who don't cheat.

10. Be Diligent in Your Field

"Do you see a man skilled in his work? He will serve before kings; he will not serve before obscure men" (Proverbs 22:29).

Every young person I have ever met has wanted to leave his or her footprints in the sand in some way. The tenth "commandment" gives a great guiding principle. The business spoken of here is probably a God-given vocation. The man or woman who finds the work assigned to him or her by God will ultimately not live in obscurity. All of us know people who are great carpenters or doctors or teachers who have embraced the call to diligence in their fields. Not only do they seem to have been created for these jobs, they carry out their service with what looks like effortless dignity. Watching them should cause all of us to give thanks to God that He truly gives individuals specific assignments in the earth.

The Right Perspective

It is important for believers who have started on the journey called "the way of the warrior" to be sure to embrace heaven's perspective of life. We are called to take strategic posts for God in the earth. David articulated it this way: "The earth is the LORD's, and everything in it, the world, and all who live in it" (Psalm 24:1).

One of the ways we maintain God's light and witness in the earth is by allowing ourselves to be positioned by God on His chessboard. Think about it this way. None of us chooses our race, our sex or our nation of origin. These starting points give a godly frame of reference.

Some of us have been born into less than desirable situations in order to give us a passion for social reform or ministry to people who share our origins. Others of us have been given fabulous starting points, like Florence Nightingale, in order to make an unusual contribution to our generation.

God needs the kings and the pawns on His chessboard. No one is insignificant. A chauffeur, like my great uncle, may influence the chairman of one of America's most powerful companies. Influence comes in all sizes and shapes. We all should consider our life's opportunities as a commission—a sacred trust. The apostle Paul made a helpful statement as he evaluated his contribution to Christ's Kingdom. This statement may also help us appreciate our unique significance before the Lord.

He wrote:

> Now it is required that those who have been given a trust must prove faithful. I care very little if I am judged by you or by any human court; indeed, I do not even judge myself. My conscience is clear, but that does not make me innocent. It is the Lord who judges me. Therefore judge nothing before the appointed time; wait till the Lord comes. He will bring to light what is hidden in darkness and will expose the motives of men's hearts. At that time each will receive his praise from God.
>
> 1 Corinthians 4:2–5

Let's allow Him to direct our steps today. Let's journey in faith on the way of the warrior, remembering that our lives are of immense, eternal significance because of Christ.

Before you charge off to change the world through wealth and influence, please take the following inventory.

TAKING INVENTORY

1. How have you balanced heart and head in your calling?
2. What impressed you the most about Florence Nightingale?
3. What moved you the most about Florence's father?
4. How was Florence's life similar to David's?
5. What is the primary anointing in your life?
6. Has God placed you somewhere for training?
7. Looking at the Ten Commandments of Influence, rate your current effectiveness in each one:
   - Release the Twin Sisters of Blessing
   - Pursue Operational Wisdom
   - Refine Godly Character
   - Train a Child
   - Set the Right Relational Atmosphere
   - Keep Your Spiritual Ears Open
   - Take Care of the Needy
   - Use Debt Strategically
   - Maintain Integrity Even When It Hurts
   - Be Diligent in Your Field
8. Looking at your evaluation above, which is your strongest commandment? Which is your weakest? What will you do as a next step to move forward toward wealth and influence?

4

Achievement

Success in the Kingdom

Potential is interesting, but performance is everything.

Coach Robert O'Dell

It had been only a couple of months since the wrestler, a college freshman, had defeated the heavyweight college champion in a regular season match. It had been an amazing victory and it had shocked everyone. The New England champion had apparently underestimated the quickness and deceptive strength of this young man from Ohio.

Today was a greater challenge. The freshman was competing in the semifinals of the New England Collegiate Wrestling Tournament. He could actually become a champion himself. His opponent was a huge wrestler from the Massachusetts Institute of Technology (MIT) who outweighed him by nearly one hundred pounds. This kind of physical mismatch was part of the challenge of the "unlimited weight" class. The mismatch in this case was not simply physical. The MIT senior was a 22-year-old, systematic wrestler who possessed everything the freshman lacked—size, experience and a great range of moves.

"Make your move, now!" the coach yelled from the sidelines. "You can do it! Use your speed!" The young wrestler circled slowly, looking for his opportunity. He was down by one point. A takedown would give him the victory and put him in the tournament finals. Only two minutes separated him from victory.

In those crucial moments, this young man as well as those who had followed his career knew that he had a chance because of the shocking outcome of that earlier match against the New England heavyweight champ. That match had not looked at all promising for the freshman because he had lost his first five collegiate outings; but, then, he had only wrestled one year in high school.

In a burst of inspiration, just two days before that momentous match, he had shaved his head bald. What a stunt! A Dartmouth wrestler had told him that it would "psyche out the enemy."

It did—and more besides. When he stepped out of the darkness into the spotlight focused on the center of the mat, the giddy, chattering crowd froze as it caught sight of him. Staring at this cross between Yul Brynner and Mr. T, everyone muttered the same question: *Who is that muscular kid?* The match began quickly with a bold lunge. It was a move that his coach had drilled him on for two months. To the young man's surprise, it worked.

Equally surprising was the reaction of the champ's home crowd. They seemed to abandon their hero with their silence. Like a fearful witness at the scene of a mugging, they hid their faces or looked away. The longer the freshman wrestled, the bolder he became. He was on a roll.

And not only did he win, his team won as well. What a turnaround! What a feeling of accomplishment!

Now he had the chance to repeat that stellar performance—and become a champion. The crowd watched breathlessly. But in a few seconds the referee blew his whistle, signaling the end of the match. It was over. He had lost.

What happened? Why had he been successful in one instance and not in another? He had made a classic mistake: He had played it too safe. He had everything he needed to win—except the confidence that he could really achieve his goal. In short, he had not really been defeated by the enemy in front of him; he had been defeated by his own fears. He had traded places emotionally with the champion he had beaten earlier in the year. He ended the year with a winning season, but he could have been the champion.

I hope that you can relate to this story. Missed opportunities are certainly part of the human condition. We can remember tests that we did not study for, businesses we should have invested in, the people we should have married and a whole host of "would-of, could-of, should-of" thoughts. This story of this freshman is very meaningful to me because I, Harry Jackson, was that kid. (And Coach O'Dell, quoted above, was one of my athletic coaches.) I learned more from that defeat than I learned from scores of victories.

I learned that fear often undermines our abilities. Fear robs us of our potential. For believers who have access to the power of God in prayer, fear does to us what kryptonite does to Superman: It destroys our strength. Then when we recover from fear's debilitating effects, we realize what could have been. It is then that we drink from the bitter cup of regret and its death-dealing effects: "Regret is the murderer of optimism and the evangelist of despair. It breeds in dark places like mold on crusted bread."[1]

Fear was not the only inhibitor of my dream for success that day. In this chapter we will discuss several obstacles on the warrior's pathway to true achievement—obstacles that you and I face every day. And we will see how David handled them, because, unlike the wrestling story I just shared with you, David's story was radically different when he faced the challenge of a lifetime. His decisions catapulted him to success and helped him fulfill his calling. We have already mentioned his battle with Goliath. I want to look at it in more depth here because it is what marked him as a champion.

First Samuel 17 catalogues the steps that David took to win this first of his greatest battles. David did not say to himself, *This will look good on my resume!* Instead he took three distinct steps: (1) He overcame fear by daring to dream, (2) he listened to the right voices and (3) he invested in his unique strengths. Let's look at each of these.

Step 1: Overcoming Fear

There are three ways that David overcame fear of Goliath—which was actually fear of death. First of all, he focused on the goal of protecting his nation. When David's oldest brother accused him of pride and wrong motives, David asked simply, "What have I now done? *Is there not a cause?*"(1 Samuel 17:29, KJV, emphasis added).

This is a very important question. David's line of reasoning went like this. *If no one else responds, my people will be defeated. It's obvious that no one else is stepping up to meet this challenge. The worst I can do is get myself killed. I would rather die trying to save the nation than live under cowardice and disgrace.* Many of us only ask the question, "What if I mess up?" Perhaps we should ask David's question, "Is there not a reason to risk one's life?" Most of us will never have to risk our natural lives for the honor of God. We may, however, have to risk our reputations or our conveniences or a little money to promote the will of God.

The second way that David overcame fear was the belief in the call of God upon his life.

David was aware that Saul's rise to the throne of Israel began with a national crisis (see 1 Samuel 11:1–11). A man named Nahash, an Ammonite, had encamped against a town called Jabesh, and the people of this region cried out for help. Nahash's name means "serpent" and this story seems to show that he came by his name honestly. Nahash offered to make peace with the nation only if the men allowed their right eyes to be thrust out, impairing their ability to fight. Upon hearing this, the Spirit of God came upon Saul, who grew angry and decided to defy his powerful foe. Saul's victory proved to the people that he was, indeed, the one whom God had anointed to be king and he was crowned shortly thereafter. Similarly, at the challenge of Goliath, David's heart leapt, and zeal for God's purposes rose up within him, demonstrating God's call upon him.

David's third but powerful antidote to fear was his expectation of personal reward for doing the right thing. Selfishness focuses only upon personal benefit; godly people achieve great rewards almost as a by-product of obeying the will of God.

David asked the men standing near him, "What will be done for the man who kills this Philistine and removes this disgrace from Israel? Who is this uncircumcised Philistine that he should defy the armies of the living God? They repeated to him what they had been saying and told him, "This is what will be done for the man who kills him."

1 Samuel 17:26–27

No wonder David in his later years passed on to younger men this observation:

I was young and now I am old, yet I have never seen the righteous forsaken or their children begging bread. They are always generous and lend freely; their children will be blessed. Turn from evil and do good; then you will dwell in the land forever.

Psalm 37:25–27

Step 2: Listening to the Right Voices

The apostle Paul made an interesting observation as he attempted to explain the supernatural gift of tongues: "There are, it may be, so many kinds of voices in the world, and none of them is without signification" (1 Corinthians 14:10, KJV). Every voice in our world has meaning, but we are not to be directed by every voice, nor are we to be distracted. Personal guidance is all about knowing what voice to listen to and how to use the information given. Listening to confusing voices can destroy our faith, conviction and obedience. In the Garden of Eden, Eve was taken in by Satan's sly phrase, *Hath God said . . . ?* (Genesis 3:1, KJV, emphasis added).

As we learn to follow the will of God, we must learn that partial obedience is still disobedience. If the enemy of our souls can get us to settle for partial obedience, he wins the war.

David needed to disregard several voices that clamored for attention. They were:

The voice of his past
The voice of his envious brothers
The voice of the fearful

If David had listened solely to the hurts of his past, he would never have discovered the champion within himself. David's past resonated with competition between him and his seven older brothers; the family chores and assignments he was given reflect a lack of respect. As a result of his background, rejection seemed to be David's emotional inheritance. Like his son Absalom, David earned approval through his good looks and his performance. Later in life, David developed the ability to lead armies and motivate men. Domestically, however, he never learned how to give his children a sense of belonging or security in his love. Someone once said, "You can't give what you never received yourself."

Sometimes it seems that our families are best at seeing our gifts without recognizing our potential. I am not sure that David's father, Jesse, ever thought that his son would amount to much. My clue to this was Jesse's response when the prophet Samuel came seeking God's choice for king from among his sons. Jesse did not even bring David into the house for Samuel to meet until the older brothers were disqualified (see 1 Samuel 16:11). Sometimes those closest to us cannot see what God is doing in our lives. Remember that many people in Jesus' hometown could see only a carpenter's son instead of the Son of God.

It is important that we receive counsel only from people who see the call of God upon our lives. Years ago, my wife and I were invited to join an informal minister's network. The group never recognized that my wife has a powerful preaching gift or a personal identity separate from mine. It seemed that every time we joined that group for fellowship, one of the leaders would repeat their initial impression of my wife as a retiring and fearful young pastor's wife with no under-standing of church life. Little wonder that they have been shocked by how well we have both done in the ministry! To choose our closest counselors from this group would have been a great mistake. Today we have accomplished much more than their vision for us could ever have encompassed.

Warriors must remember that times of inactivity may be moments in which the Lord is attempting to deepen our communion with Him. Warriors must also under-stand that we learn important lessons (like hearing God's voice) in times of peace so that we know how to act in times of war.

Step 3: Investing in Your Unique Strengths

One of the most compelling aspects of the David and Goliath story is the description of David trying on Saul's armor. Imagine this brawny teenager attempting to wear the armor of his own nation's giant (1 Samuel 10:23 tells us that Saul was a head taller than anyone else) while preparing to fight the Philistines' giant (Goliath was possibly over eleven feet tall).

> "The LORD who delivered me from the paw of the lion and the paw of the bear will deliver me from the hand of this Philistine." Saul said to David, "Go, and the LORD be with you." Then Saul dressed David in his own tunic. He put a coat of armor on him and a bronze helmet on his head. David fastened on his sword over the tunic

and tried walking around, because he was not used to them. "I cannot go in these," he said to Saul, "because I am not used to them." So he took them off. Then he took his staff in his hand, chose five smooth stones from the stream, put them in the pouch of his shepherd's bag and, with his sling in his hand, approached the Philistine. Meanwhile, the Philistine, with his shield bearer in front of him, kept coming closer to David.

1 Samuel 17:37–41

Many people do not realize that David actually put on Saul's armor. At first, he attempted to do what everyone else does: use successful methods of the past to handle today's problems. But he could not work with it. Though this picture does not describe David's age or size, I imagine a junior high kid—135 pounds soaking wet—putting on Mean Joe Green's shoulder pads and pants. The pants won't stay up and the shoulder pads are falling off. Then, they give him Mean Joe's helmet. He puts it on and takes two steps. The helmet slides around and now he is looking out of the ear hole. Next, the coach screams, "Okay, kid, we're sending you into the game!"

This is what happened to David. He was trying to fit in. He was trying to use conventional wisdom. The armor provided protection and strength for Saul, but it was not David's strength. David made a choice. He decided to invest in his unique abilities, his own strengths, rather than Saul's.

David picked up five stones. Then he packed them in a certain way. This was a methodical preparation. If I were going to war and I had just one weapon, I don't think I would pack just one clip of bullets. I would have clips strapped on copiously to be prepared for anything. David knew he could get the giant with one stone. He knew if Goliath had his shield up, he might need a second stone. But because David had practiced day after day on the backside of the mountain, he knew he would not need more than five stones. He knew what his skill was; he knew what his gifting was; he knew what his anointing was.

And he achieved his goal. Goliath lay slain and David was one huge step closer to his calling as king.

Obeying the Master's Voice

This story of one of David's greatest achievements helps us understand the meaning of his powerful singing meditation later in his life: "Even though I walk through the valley of the shadow of death, I will fear no evil, for you are with me; your rod and your staff, they comfort me" (Psalm 23:4).

The rod and staff were shepherds' tools, allowing them to guide and protect the sheep, particularly those who decided to ignore their master's voice and go their own way. And as Scripture points out all too clearly, we, like sheep, have all gone astray. We fail to obey God's direction for our lives and wonder why success eludes us.

The idea of listening personally for the voice of the Lord can be challenging to some Christian traditionalists. In the King James Version of the Bible, however, there are five references that include the phrase "the voice of the LORD." The first is a prophetic message from the Lord spoken to Israel through the prophet Samuel. It says essentially, "I'm giving in to your carnal request for a king, yet the LORD will meet you even in this institution if you will obey His voice" (see 1 Samuel 12:13–14). Samuel then added: "But if ye will not obey the voice of the LORD, but rebel against the commandment of the LORD, then shall the hand of the LORD be against you, as it was against your fathers" (verse 15, KJV). The other four of these references to "the voice of the LORD" deal with Saul's disobedience to the Lord's direct commands.

One example of Saul's failure to obey was when God gave him the command to utterly destroy the "wicked" Amalekites and everything belonging to them. When the Lord speaks, He expects to be obeyed. Saul and the Israelites did not obey; they spared the life of the king and kept the best of the livestock. The verses below— Samuel's confronting Saul—give a view of the Lord's perspective on obedience to His voice:

> And Samuel said, Hath the LORD as great delight in burnt offerings and sacrifices, as in obeying the voice of the LORD? Behold, to obey is better than sacrifice, and to hearken than the fat of rams. For rebellion is as the sin of witchcraft, and stubbornness is as iniquity and idolatry. Because thou hast rejected the word of the LORD, he hath also rejected thee from being king.
>
> 1 Samuel 15:22–23, KJV

In Saul and David's day, just like ours, the only way to stay in God's good graces was through personal obedience. Mature Christians should respond to the Lord's directives like willing warriors in battle rather than meandering children who may lose their mother's note on the way to the grocery store.

We must be committed to the confirmable directives of the Holy Spirit to our hearts. These directives may come from the specific commandments and principles found in Scripture, the inner voice of the Holy Spirit and the voice of our consciences before God.

Sacrificing Our Own Plans

Rebellion is not just disobedience to God's specific direction. Rebellion is also in operation when we do not wait for His direction and charge ahead on our own.

This happens when we make up agendas not sanctioned by God and use our time, talents and treasures to pay for them.

It is natural to want to achieve. In fact, every believer is destined to walk in a sphere of victory. The hard part comes in realizing that many of those victories lie on the other side of personal valleys of death—often death of agendas that block our paths like enormous Goliaths. Both young and old struggle with obstacles, but I am finding that our God-given dreams and the corresponding courage it takes to pursue them are quicker to die as we grow older. Unless we focus unerringly on the glory of God, putting aside our self-centered agendas, we will be unable to use either the strength of youth or the wisdom of age.

We learn once again from Saul's grave mistakes. First Samuel 13:4–15 shows what happens when we take our own course of action without waiting for the Lord's voice. In these verses, Saul chose not to wait for the prophet Samuel to fulfill the duties of priest and prophet and took matters into his own hands.

It was during a national crisis. Saul had waited seven days for Samuel to come and bless him and his troops by making an offering to God. Thirty thousand Philistines were set in battle array at a place called Gilgal. They could have attacked Saul at any time.

This situation was not at all like Saul's first wartime experience, which we discussed earlier in this chapter, when divine guidance from God came upon him and his zeal for God moved him to challenge the enemies of Israel at Jabesh (see 1 Samuel 11:5–9). This time Saul was overcome with fear. He was especially worried because the Israelites, who had gathered at Gilgal, were getting nervous. He did not want to lose face or destroy their morale. Thus, he let his sense of urgency, motivated by fear, lead him into sin. The New Testament is clear about this kind of action: "Everything that does not come from faith is sin" (Romans 14:23).

Saul could not afford a battlefield mistake in this situation, but he could also not afford a spiritual mistake. He should have viewed himself as a servant of the Lord who needed a directive for this occasion. Historically, time and time again, Israel defeated superior, hostile foes by receiving and following a word from God. Saul was well aware of the stories of Moses, Joshua and judges like Gideon and Deborah, but it is easier to pay lip service to dependence upon God than it is to live it.

Saul chose to act. He did not wait for Samuel to arrive and make the sacrifice; he did it himself, a direct violation of God's ordinances. God called Saul's actions "sin" and Samuel spoke these prophetic words:

> "You acted foolishly," Samuel said. "You have not kept the command the LORD your God gave you; if you had, he would have established your kingdom over Israel for all time. But now your kingdom will not endure; the LORD has sought out a man after his own heart and appointed him leader of his people, because you have not kept the LORD's command."
>
> 1 Samuel 13:13–14

David was that man after God's heart—that king who sought the Lord for direction in crisis situations instead of acting independently.

Years ago, I was struggling with a major issue of guidance for our local church. I really did not know what to do. In other words, I did not have a directive from the Lord. My elders were also in conflict concerning our specific course of action. I desperately did not want to "mess up." The longer this situation continued, the more worried I became. I had two choices: I could move ahead on my own initiative or I could simply rest in what I knew God had spoken up to that point and wait for further clarification of His will.

I am grateful to say that I decided to wait, and in that waiting I learned the assurance that comes from resting in the Lord's timing. Plus, His answer was better than anything I could have conjured up.

My mentor, Judson Cornwall, gave me an excellent explanation of how to remain obedient to the will of God. He reminded me on many occasions that the Lord must initiate direction. It is God's job to make His will known. "Big decisions," he told me, "require big guidance. We must function like firemen who do all the daily chores without hesitation, but we can respond to a fire alarm only when one has been issued. Rest until you get direct orders, and then obey them explicitly."

Benefits Will Come

We talked about prosperity in the last chapter, but I want to give an interesting definition of it here. *Prosperity* can be defined as "the ability to complete one's assignment." Jesus told us to seek first the Kingdom of God and all these things will be added to us (see Matthew 6:33). The residual benefit of obedience to the will of God may well be having our needs met and enjoying some of our great dreams.

I want to mention Dennis Bakke in this regard. He fights the Goliaths of greed and cynicism in American business and shows that God blesses us with success when we obey His commands. Bakke is a Harvard MBA who thinks like David. He decided to use his training to craft a company built on Kingdom paradigms, and the results have been astounding.

AES Corp. is probably the biggest company that nobody has ever heard of. With 118 power plants in 16 countries, the power supplier based in Arlington, Virginia, is one of the world's largest providers of electricity, boasting a market capitalization of about $14 billion. With 40,000 employees worldwide, the Bible-believing, evangelical Bakke is literally changing the world in the name of Christ.

In a press conference some years ago in Brazil, Bakke was describing the purpose of his company. The conference was held at the time of Mother Teresa's death. With godly inspiration, Bakke placed the celebrated nun's picture on the podium and discussed his concept that businesses exist to help a community, not to strip it. He also shared his company's concept of the value of people, and how that is lived out in the "decentralization" of the company's structure. The newspapers covered his presentation positively, but the headlines showed the often-misunderstood position of godly dealings in today's secular world. One read: "Christian or Communist?"

The world may not know how to label the revolutionary works that you and I accomplish for Christ, but Mr. Bakke has shown us that God undergirds and causes to prosper the work He calls us to perform.

Isaiah's words have rung in my ears for years as I think about not only my personal life but the destiny of the United States: "'If you are willing and obedient, you will eat the best from the land; but if you resist and rebel, you will be devoured by the sword.' For the mouth of the LORD has spoken" (Isaiah 1:19–20).

Like our modern-day champions, David was willing and obedient. His life was marked by the discipline of prayer and praise. The years that David spent tending the sheep were not wasted because that was where he learned how to walk with God, to hear from God. The description of David as "the sweet psalmist of Israel"

(2 Samuel 23:1, KJV) shows the kind of intimacy David had with his Lord.

When you are challenged by a Goliath in your path, here are three points to remember:

1. God does not call the qualified; He qualifies the called.
2. Perfection is not necessary—or even possible. But God does require willingness.
3. Servanthood is the best motivation for achievement and success.

David was not perfect, which is encouraging for the rest of us. He succeeded not because he was someone special but because he followed godly steps to achievement and success. In fact, his life helps us remember that it is the ordinary people that God wants for warriors—the ones out tending sheep, the ones put down by "more mature" brothers, the ones who are not big enough to wear the king's armor. David was not perfect, but he waited for God's direction and then he was obedient. If we hope to achieve great things for God, we must do the same.

Now, let's review.

TAKING INVENTORY

Look at your life in terms of how you have faced the following:

1. Overcoming Fear
   - Like the author, where have you achieved "the impossible" against overwhelming odds? Did you sense the hand of God at work?

- Like David, have you faced a fear that others could not face?

2. Listening to the Right Voices
   - Does your family history bring voices to your head that motivate you toward the Lord's destiny or away from it?
   - Do you choose the right counselors who recognize your call and gift?

3. Investing in Your Unique Strengths
   - Do you regularly pray and praise in order to strengthen yourself for battles you will face in the future?
   - Does God give you specific preparation for battles you face?

4. Remembering the Way God Calls People
   - God does not call the qualified; He qualifies the called.
   - Perfection is not necessary—or even possible. But God does require willingness.
   - Servanthood is the best motivation for achievement and success.

5. Of these four principles, which does God need most to work into your heart?

5

Righteousness

Becoming a Voice, Not an Echo

Justice is like the Kingdom of God—it is not without us as a fact, it is within us as a great yearning.

George Eliot

It was December 5, 1955, and the first mass meeting of the Montgomery Improvement Association (MIA) was about to begin. As the crowd of thousands gathered, the noise was deafening. Everyone wondered what Dr. Martin Luther King Jr. would say. After all, Rosa Parks had just refused to sit in the back of the bus in a heroic act of civil disobedience. The four days since Parks' act of defiance had seemed like an eternity. As newly elected association president, King would have to set the right tone for the organization's sake and the city's safety.

Dr. King usually took days to develop his powerful messages. For this meeting, however, he did not have the luxury of extended preparation. Instead he drew from the deepest foundations of his faith. King was aware that any candid discussion of racial problems in Montgomery, Alabama, could get out of hand. He did not want to ignite bitter, violent outbursts. Dr. King knew that forgiveness and love were great values to draw upon; in fact, he was a great advocate of non-violence. Yet he must have asked himself the question, *How can someone change the violent South?*

There was no doubt that he had seen black men hanging from trees, having been mutilated, tortured and lynched. Some people called these acts the "strange fruit of the South." King was very aware that separate was "not quite equal" for blacks versus whites in the South. Every black person he knew was tired of being second class, tired of being disrespected. King knew that something had to change. He knew he was the man, and he knew the time was now.

The MIA proceedings began with two hymns: "Onward, Christian Soldiers" and "Leaning on the Everlasting Arms." Then King began by appealing to the faith of the African-American community despite the fact that blacks in Montgomery faced a secular problem. In addition, he encouraged his listeners to believe in the power of biblical justice. King's sermon went one step further than most sermons of that day. He encouraged the association to act on its belief in divine justice and the American tradition of legal protest. He challenged the members to turn their beliefs into practical, positive action. The Montgomery Bus Boycott began.

For the next month, King received thirty to forty threatening letters and phone calls a day. Imagine going through the Christmas season with threats that you and your young family might not live to see the new year arrive. Then one night a phone call stood out from the others. In *Stride Towards Freedom*, King wrote that he received an ominous phone call just as he was about to doze off to sleep. The caller promised that before seven days had passed, King would be sorry that he ever came to Montgomery. King, by his own admission, was afraid. He got up and offered a desperate prayer from his kitchen table. But in the midst of his fear, he felt as though he could hear an inner voice saying, *Stand up for righteousness, stand up for truth; and God will be at your side forever.*

King's uncertainty disappeared. Three days later his house was firebombed. Steadied by his "kitchen prayer," he preached boldly to the crowd that gathered outside of his badly damaged house that they must love their enemies. He sent them home on fire with love and faith instead of a call to arms, riot or violent retaliation.

We celebrate Dr. King's birthday because his courage and resolve advanced civil justice for blacks. His life was also a gift to all Americans. Today, his dream is a living legacy, which is still changing the nation. He was a true spiritual warrior.

In an irony only the Lord could produce, the same city from which the telegraph message originated to begin the Civil War, a spiritual telegraph was sent to begin the civil rights movement. Montgomery, Alabama, would become a place where healing and justice would spring forth. Today the Rosa Parks Museum stands just down the street from the Dexter Avenue Baptist Church once pastored by Martin Luther King Jr. A breach in history was healed because of the work of the Holy Spirit and the obedience of a true spiritual warrior.

Practical Glory

As people positioned by God in strategic places, all believers are charged with the task of increasing the rule and reign of the Lord in the earth. Although He is the true ruler of all, His dominion is visible only where believers live under the authority of their heavenly King. Omnipotent and omniscient, God chose to work through men and women. No wonder Paul declared in Romans 8:19 that "the creation waits in eager expectation for the sons of God to be revealed."

Everyone has experienced unfairness and hypocrisy. These are instances in which Christ's Kingdom is *not* being made manifest. His Kingdom is seen through the power of the Holy Spirit or the fruit of mature Christian character.

Justice is a major manifestation of God's character and virtue. This chapter explains in concrete ways the believer's responsibility to be an instrument of God's justice. The scriptural basis for this conclusion is Psalm 101, which gives us insight into David's theology of divine justice. Three guidelines are given in this psalm that need to be lived out in our lives: (1) God's loyal love and justice are the basis for our relationship with Him (see verse 1); (2) it is our responsibility to reflect these values in our actions and in our spheres of responsibility (see verse 2); and (3) personal integrity is where justice begins (see verses 3–8).

Let's take a look at each of these.

1. God's Loyal Love and Justice

No one ever gets exactly what he deserves. Every one of us has broken the rules of both God and man, for which we should have been punished. The life-changing aspect of Christianity is that the blood of Jesus was spilled to erase eternal penalties for our sins. The brutal execution of Christ on the cross was a substitutionary work that expunged our spiritual records in heaven's courts.

Romans 5:17 says that we have been given a "gift of righteousness" because of the work of Christ on the cross. Now God, in His mercy, forgives our sins and treats us as though we are totally righteous. Then He goes even farther by creating an atmosphere of authority around our lives, a grace bubble, if you will. As people come into contact with us, they see the Lord of the universe protect us and make judgments for us according to His holiness. In other words, if a thief tries to steal from us, God punishes him for attacking us. In Genesis 12, the Abrahamic covenant says something remarkable about this man who was given the Old Testament version of the "gift of righteousness": "I will bless those who bless you, and whoever curses you I will curse; and all peoples on earth will be blessed through you" (Genesis 12:3). As Abraham's spiritual descendants, this covenant becomes ours as well.

No wonder David sang to the Lord in worship about Jehovah's amazing mercy and justice operating in his life. Listen to these words: "I will sing of your love and justice; to you, O LORD, I will sing praise" (Psalm 101:1).

The way God creates deeper holiness in us is through revealing His love and mercy to us *before* we measure up. Like someone giving a down payment on a purchase, God often reaches out to us and then calls us to Himself. We must remember that His kindness leads us to repentance (see Romans 2:4).

Once we have experienced the reality of the love of God, we become responsible to act as true representatives of God, demonstrating His love and justice in the earth on behalf of others. We are to become peacemakers and those who bring the glory of God into the lives of others. This is the next guideline.

2. Our Reciprocal Responsibility

One of the most powerful books I have read in the last few years is *The Jewish Phenomenon: Seven Keys to the Enduring Wealth of a People* by Steven Silberger (Longstreet Press, 2000). The book explains seven major strategies the Jewish community has used to influence the world despite its minority status. This influence may be partially natural or material, but has its basis in spiritual principles and philosophical militancy and serves as a guide for those who seek justice. I call the approach introduced here "God's blueprint for dominion." As we reflect His justice and righteousness, He works through us to bring about change on the earth.

Many scholars say that the Hebrew word for charity is *tzedakah*, from a root word meaning "justice" or "righteousness." Both David of old and his modern Jewish descendants have maintained the idea that a truly righteous person helps create an atmosphere of social justice for the needy and vulnerable. Moses Maimonides, a 12th-century Jewish rabbi and philosopher, enunciated eight levels of tzedakah. The levels are fascinating. Please note that Maimonides wrote these in the context of supporting fellow Jews financially, but his ultimate goal was social justice. Here are the levels:

1. The person gives grudgingly.
2. The person gives graciously, even happily.
3. The person gives, but only after being asked.
4. The person gives before being asked.
5. The person does not know the recipient, but the recipient knows the benefactor.
6. The person knows the recipient, but the recipient does not know the benefactor.

7. The person does not know the recipient, and the recipient does not know the benefactor.

8. The person helps another by enabling that person to become self-sufficient through an interest-free loan, a business partnership or help in gaining a skill or finding employment.[1]

Modern Jews are transforming their world with random acts of kindness as they live out biblically based virtue, including tzedakah. In *Worth* magazine's 1999 list of top philanthropists, for example, out of one hundred names, 35 are Jewish.[2] Steve Silberger states: "Jews are taught that charity is an obligation rooted in social justice, not love or pity for their fellow man."[3] In light of this explanation of what it means to be righteous, these righteous ones can become cultural change agents.

As I meditated on this concept of righteousness, I realized the significance of the Lord's statement to Abraham about the wicked city of Sodom, which He was poised to destroy: "If I find fifty righteous people in the city of Sodom, I will spare the whole place for their sake" (Genesis 18:26). At Abraham's respectful insistence, the Lord agreed to lower the number: If He could find even ten righteous men in the city, He would show mercy to all (see verse 32).

Ten men with the righteousness approach of Moses Maimonides could have transformed one of the most corrupt communities in biblical history. Righteous citizens can truly become salt and light in our world as well. They do not have to begin as official community leaders or politicians. In fact, David said that justice must start at home: "I will be careful to lead a blameless life—when will you come to me? I will walk in my house with blameless heart" (Psalm 101:2). The sheer force of a godly lifestyle can shift the culture and stay the judgment of God. Modern-day Sodoms like New York City or Los Angeles need just a few good men and women to reflect God's justice and righteousness. No, I am not talking about the U.S. military. We are discussing the army of the Lord.

The 21st-century Church is under tremendous siege by the culture. As a result of the constant assault against our beliefs and principles, our concept of righteousness has started to center solely around personal holiness and our personal standing before God. By that I mean we have begun to evaluate righteousness in terms of the negatives we avoid instead of the power we were meant to create in the earth. Psalm 89:14 says that "righteousness and justice are the foundation" of God's throne. In other words, God's power will truly be demonstrated when personal righteousness is embraced and an atmosphere of social justice is created.

America's first Great Awakening occurred when John and Charles Wesley preached salvation along with abolition of slavery. This message was a major aspect of the revival of the 1740s. What is missing among evangelicals in our day is the commitment to create justice and to make the lives of our fellow man better as an expression of our faith. Social justice is clearly the missing ingredient.

The Bible has much to say about justice. Sometimes the concept of justice is obscured by the translator's choice of English words. The King James Bible, for instance, uses many words that have obscure or arcane meanings today. One of those funny words is *judgment* in relation to God's daily dealings with His people. When I read the word *judgment*, I think about God dressed in black with a big old stick. It seems almost as if God's going to hit somebody over the head—or worse, maybe open the earth and send folks sliding into the abyss. In reality, the word *judgment* implies adjudication, or God setting things in order.

If you look at a modern translation, such as the New International Version, you find that the word *justice* is substituted often for the word *judgment*. And the word *justice* has a very different meaning, doesn't it? Most Americans think about getting justice as having our day in court, when we finally appear before the judge who can put an end to our disputes. The incredible number of courtroom shows on television suggests that people are obsessed with getting justice. They are even willing to be publicly humiliated on television to get a speedy verdict. Yet, despite the popular clamor today for personal justice, I am convinced that the justice God wants us to pursue involves the oppressed and victimized.

The call for Christians, then, is to become people who promote, release and create justice. As we look at creating and producing justice, let's consider Psalm 82:3: "Defend the cause of the weak and fatherless; maintain the rights of the poor and oppressed." The Lord seems to emphasize to us that we have a responsibility to carry out justice as a way of glorifying Him. We can ensure that we get justice by creating it for someone else.

Heaven's courts always pay attention to injustice. And the Lord honors His unique club of spiritual "men in black." In fact, He would rather we worship Him by serving others in our circle of influence than by simply repeating religious statements of worship in our gatherings Sunday morning. Solomon summarized this point for everyday people: "To do what is right and just is more acceptable to the LORD than sacrifice" (Proverbs 21:3).

3. Personal Integrity: Gateway to the Nations

God desires that people show His heart and character in the earth in practical ways. Every day, people can change their world. David gives us his personal formula for transforming the world in the remainder of Psalm

101. Let's read the final six verses of this passage in the New American Standard Bible.

> I will set no worthless thing before my eyes; I hate the work of those who fall away; it shall not fasten its grip on me. A perverse heart shall depart from me; I will know no evil. Whoever secretly slanders his neighbor, him I will destroy; no one who has a haughty look and an arrogant heart will I endure. My eyes shall be upon the faithful of the land, that they may dwell with me; he who walks in a blameless way is the one who will minister to me. He who practices deceit shall not dwell within my house; he who speaks falsehood shall not maintain his position before me. Every morning I will destroy all the wicked of the land, so as to cut off from the city of the LORD all those who do iniquity.
>
> Psalm 101:3–8

I have summarized David's thoughts from Psalm 101:3–8 in six steps that could change our world. Each of these points will help us fulfill God's mandate for righteousness and justice.

1. Watch what you meditate upon.

The old adage says, "You are what you eat." Just as true is the fact that you and I are affected by what we meditate upon. What I watch on television, the Internet and in person, therefore, affects my thinking. We must be disciplined about what we allow to come into our eyes and our ears.

2. Choose close associates carefully.

Our close friends are another major influence in our lives. Like people affected by secondhand smoke, our associates' actions can easily rub off on us.

3. Confront people who lack personal integrity.

David is advocating that we confront people who violate confidences and speak disparagingly of our close friends, fellow church members and business associates.

Proverbs 16:28 warns us that a whisperer separates even the closest friends. Further, some people in the Body of Christ have developed the bad habit of cynically critiquing and criticizing Christian leaders. The unity of the Body of Christ must be protected actively.

4. Develop a list of role models.

All of us have people we admire. We should pray for them and follow the example they give to us. One of my friends, for instance, has done a great job of disciplining herself to fast and pray. In the areas of prayer and fasting, I allow myself to be shaped and influenced greatly by this person. I celebrate and draw from her strength. On the other hand, I pray for her in the areas of her weaknesses that she has shared with me.

5. Get counsel only from those who walk the talk.

Everyone needs trusted counselors and friends. As I talk about my battles with confidants, I must make a distinction between those I talk to for support and those I talk to for counsel.

6. Every day be vigilant to extend the Kingdom of God by repeating the first five steps.

As a final word, let's remember that great blessing comes to us when we learn to distill provocative principles down into specific steps of action. The prophet Micah said it best as he talked about God's requirements for us: "He has showed you, O man, what is good. And what does the LORD require of you? To act justly and to love mercy and to walk humbly with your God" (Micah 6:8).

TAKING INVENTORY

1. What are some ways that you see the "sons of God being revealed" (see Romans 8:19) in our unrighteous world?

2. Have you had the experience of pursuing justice in the face of fear? What helped you?

3. How well do you think the Church is doing on the following aspects of justice from Psalm 101? How do you live up to these?
   - God's loyal love and justice are the basis of our relationship with Him.
   - It is our responsibility to reflect these values in our actions and in our spheres of responsibility.
   - Personal integrity is where justice begins.

4. Evaluate your practice of giving, as it relates to Christian values, according to tzedakah. How do you give of your time and talents for the cause of justice?
   - Reluctantly?
   - Graciously?
   - Only when asked?
   - Before being asked?
   - Without knowing who will receive your gift, while the recipient knows of your identity?
   - Knowing who will receive your gift, but without making your own identity known?
   - Not knowing who will receive your gift, and without your identity being made known?
   - In a way that enables another to become self-sufficient through a loan, or helping him or her gain a skill or find employment?

5. From David's example, pray over the following and ask the Lord daily to continue your process of growth in each area.
   - Watch what you meditate upon.
   - Choose close associates carefully.
   - Confront people who lack personal integrity.
   - Develop a list of role models.
   - Get counsel only from those who walk the talk.

6

Reflection

Thinking like Jesus

A good Christian useth the world for his necessity, but his main work is to draw near to God.

Thomas Watson

I was having a hard time getting my notes together for my Fourth of July message. It was different the year before. That message, preached at a nearby retreat center, became the talk of the week. In fact, the heart of my speech became the core of an article that was published in a national Christian magazine.

My speech had been a reverent but entertaining moment in the program.

The evening had included music with a patriotic theme, fireworks, food and games for the children. For most of us the celebration of our nation's founding always revolved around harmless family fun—nothing else. Perhaps the fact that the owner of the retreat center was a relatively recent European immigrant gave the proceedings an air of solemnity.

This year I was distracted. As I prayed about some of the social problems of the nation, I began to weep. This was quite a new experience for me. Sobbing, I asked the Lord to give me a platform to speak about these issues. For a year and a half I had been doing research on the black church and its contribution to our American society. I felt that I had a lot to say but I did not know when, where or how to say it. Over the next few days my inarticulate sobs turned into a pivotal, strategic prayer. I began to ask God for free time on a Christian radio.

In just a little over four weeks, I was offered a free half-hour radio program, five days a week. It was a tangible opportunity to share my ideas within the most powerful city in the world—Washington, D.C. So I began experimenting with our church's daily radio program. It became a substantial Christian talk program almost overnight. Within six weeks I was integrally involved in a major summit for African-American pastors, which addressed just a few of the issues on my heart.

During that pastors' summit, I began to understand that the political process in the nation is an important aspect of our culture and that the Church in America has abdicated a great deal of its authority because of ignorance and fear. Jesus would not have made excuses for the 21st-century involvement of His Church in the national political debate.

"You are the light of the world. A city on a hill cannot be hidden" (Matthew 5:14) would have been His direct words to the Church in our day. I especially realized that there was a need for the Church to engage the culture more than ever before.

These old words had become new thoughts to me. I was beginning to think like Jesus in this particular arena. The remainder of this chapter will deal with how we renew our minds so that we can be more effective in our service to God. Further, we will discuss the need for biblical meditation in order to stay sharp and full of faith.

Reprogramming the Human Computer

Spiritual warriors must reflect on both their understanding of the Scriptures and the needs of the culture. It is not enough for ministers to exegete or thoroughly analyze the Scriptures. They also must exegete their communities and culture.

Because thought-life determines actions, finding a way to keep one's thinking clear and more focused on the purposes of God will bring a more substantial impact on the world. I think of David in this regard, retreating from the complex needs of the palace by returning to the simplicity of life in the pasture.

In our generation the question is simple. If we think like Jesus, aren't we more likely to act like Jesus? The answer is yes. Although a great deal has been stated about what Jesus would do in certain circumstances, the real key to being Christlike is based on understanding how He would perceive and respond to our world.

George Barna did an excellent job in his book *Think Like Jesus*[1] in laying out a general biblical worldview based on answering seven questions. All seven questions are presuppositions. The way we answer these questions determines whether or not we will have a biblical foundation for our public policies or personal philosophies. Barna's questions are as follows:

Does God really exist?
What is the character of God?

How and why was the world created?
What is the nature and character of man?
What happens after we die?
What spiritual authorities exist?
What is truth?

In an increasingly secular America, we will find our-selves addressing these suppositional questions over and over again. On several PBS radio interviews, I found myself indirectly discussing the question of "What is truth?" with some of the most degreed people I have ever met. Unless Christians have a biblical worldview and learn to instruct non-Christians in the ultimate value of this kind of thinking, we will lose the battle of ideas in the culture.

This process is not difficult. Our minds must be thoroughly renewed by the Word of God. Then as our general biblical worldview comes into sharper focus, we can move toward the specific aspects of our lives. Take as an example the battle of ideas over same-sex marriage. The debate over this specific issue would be won easily if questions four and seven were looked at honestly.

Meditative Thought through Scripture

How did Jesus think like Jesus?
George Barna helps us understand the four elements that must come together to help us think more like Jesus. He said, "First, He had a foundation that was clear, re-liable, and accessible. Second, He maintained a laser beam focus on God's will. Third, He evaluated all infor-mation and experiences through a filter that produced appropriate choices. Fourth, He acted in faith."[2]

Along with these important elements for establishing a framework for apologetics and debate for Christians, there is another dimension of Christlike thought that comes from meditation upon the Scriptures. Faith is also released as we see things from God's perspective. As we think like Jesus and mediate upon His Word, faith comes alive in our hearts.

The psalms are classic tools for meditation, of course. David's and others' courage, vision and faith as expressed in the lovely songs help our hearts express our own longings and fears and praises. There are three kinds of biblical, Christian meditative thought expressed in the psalms. Let's look at each of these with specific scriptural examples.

1. Gaining Discipline through Recitation

The first dimension of meditation is seen in Psalm 63:6. David says: "When I remember You on my bed, I meditate on You in the night watches" (NASB). The word used here for *meditate* is *hagah*. It describes verbally reciting, muttering or speaking the Word of God. Memorization of Scripture may be the first step in this kind of meditation. Psalm 63 is a guideline for interactive, biblical meditation.

Psalm 1 uses the same Hebrew word for *meditation*. Let's look at several verses in which the psalmist describes the long-term benefits of this kind of prayer:

Blessed is the man who does not walk in the counsel of the wicked or stand in the way of sinners or sit in the seat of mockers. But his delight is in the law of the LORD, and on his law he *meditates* day and night. He is like a tree planted by streams of water, which yields its fruit in season and whose leaf does not wither. Whatever he does prospers. Not so the wicked! They are like chaff that the wind blows away. . . . For the LORD watches over the way of the righteous, but the way of the wicked will perish.

Psalm 1:1–6, emphasis added

Progressively stronger and deeper faith is developed as this discipline is used.

2. Focusing Your Thoughts with a Purpose

The second meditation technique is described in Psalms 5 and 39. The Hebrew word is *hagiyg*. Here David implies a more cerebral or mental process.

Psalm 2:1 shows that this type of focused meditation can be used—in a negative sense. The psalmist says: "Why do the nations conspire and the peoples plot in vain?" The King James Version uses the word *imagine* in place of *plot*. In other words, the heathens were scheming, devising, discussing and imagining that their negative wishes will come to pass.

The process in a positive sense seems similar to Philippians 4:8: "Finally, brothers, whatever is true, whatever is noble, whatever is right, whatever is pure, whatever is lovely, whatever is admirable—if anything is excellent or praiseworthy—think about such things."

In Psalm 5 David gives us an example of positive, focused meditation on the help that he expects to receive from God because of who God is:

Give ear to my words, O LORD, consider my sighing. Listen to my cry for help, my King and my God, for to you I pray. In the morning, O LORD, you hear my voice; in the morning I lay my requests before you and wait in expectation. You are not a God who takes pleasure in evil; with you the wicked cannot dwell. The arrogant cannot stand in your presence; you hate all who do wrong. You destroy those who tell lies; bloodthirsty and deceitful

— 89 —

men the LORD abhors. But I, by your great mercy, will
come into your house; in reverence will I bow down
toward your holy temple. Lead me, O LORD, in your
righteousness because of my enemies—make straight
your way before me.

Psalm 5:1–8

3. Combining Elements of Worship

The third approach to meditation combines the mental focus of words with the heart focus of music. The
"sweet psalmist of Israel" was not a starry-eyed dreamer
caught up in emotional fervor. As David sang and worshiped God, he fueled his spiritual vision and faith.

In Psalm 18, David gives us a feel for the kind of
meditative worship that will keep our minds stayed on
the Lord (see Isaiah 26:3, KJV). Notice the strong visual
components that ignite his praise and thanksgiving.
The introduction to the psalm says: "[David] sang to the
LORD the words of this song when the LORD delivered
him from the hand of all his enemies and from the hand
of Saul."

I love you, O LORD, my strength. The LORD is my rock,
my fortress and my deliverer; my God is my rock, in
whom I take refuge. He is my shield and the horn of
my salvation, my stronghold. I call to the LORD, who is
worthy of praise, and I am saved from my enemies. The
cords of death entangled me; the torrents of destruction
overwhelmed me. The cords of the grave coiled around
me; the snares of death confronted me. In my distress I
called to the LORD; I cried to my God for help. From his
temple he heard my voice; my cry came before him, into
his ears. The earth trembled and quaked, and the foundations of the mountains shook; they trembled because
he was angry. Smoke rose from his nostrils; consuming
fire came from his mouth, burning coals blazed out of

it. He parted the heavens and came down; dark clouds were under his feet.

Psalm 18:1–9

Examples to Follow

Throughout the Scriptures, the Lord gives us samplings from the lives of men and women who learned to think like Him, even people who lived centuries before He entered our world as our Savior! David was one of them. He loved the Law; he let the Word of God shape his worldview; and he explored the different levels of meditation so that he might give to God and receive from Him in return.

We must learn to do the same. We must think like Jesus. How? By devouring the Scriptures. In addition, we can make sure that we know the answers to suppositional questions that will be topics of debate in this generation. Then meditation—rekindling the lost art of memorizing Scripture, focusing on what is good and worshiping God—will move us to new realms of faith.

Before we go on to the next chapter to explore the power of prayer, let's take a moment to complete a spiritual inventory of our thought-lives.

TAKING INVENTORY

1. Have you ever experienced a time when God brought new understanding to old principles by highlighting their relevance to the world around you? When something like this happens, how do you respond: in obedience or in doubt?
2. Have you been asked about social or political issues by non-Christians? Have you found yourself able to give biblically based answers?

3. How well are you prepared to answer George Barna's foundational questions? Look up Scriptures for each of the following and practice your answers.
   - Does God really exist?
   - What is the character of God?
   - How and why was the world created?
   - What is the nature and character of man?
   - What happens after we die?
   - What spiritual authorities exist?
   - What is truth?

4. Are you prepared to think like Jesus? Is your foundation for God's truth clear, reliable and accessible? Are you doggedly focused on God's will? Do you evaluate all information and experiences through a filter that produces appropriate choices? Do you act in faith?

5. Reflect on the three types of meditation. Do you use these in your devotional time regularly?
   - *Hagah*—verbally reciting, muttering or speaking the Word of God
   - *Hagiyg*—a cerebral or mental process with a particular focus
   - Worship—words and music combined to give praise and receive peace

7

Intercession

Learning to Pray with Authority

Prayer enlarges the heart until it is capable of containing God's gift of himself.

Mother Teresa

Mary was one of the brightest young women I had ever met. Sharp and articulate, she was brimming with potential. As a new Christian, she hungered for the Scriptures and was fascinated by the reality of God in everyday life. To say that she had a contagious Christian walk would be putting it mildly. Other college-aged kids were drawn to her.

Surprising to me, she had grown up with an insensitive mother and a physically abusive father. Add to that the squalor and overcrowded conditions of the New York neighborhood of her origin and her life felt suffocating. The "Big Apple" is a dream location for many young people; for Mary, it was no promised land. When she was old enough to leave home, she relocated to our sleepy town in western New York and moved in with her Aunt Millie. Her aunt led her to Christ and together they began to follow an intense discipleship program. Both aunt and niece were becoming models of faith and commitment.

Then her world fell apart.

I will never forget the day Mary told me about her illness. Her words were clear and direct: "The doctor told me that I have ten tumors the size of golf balls inside of me." She blurted out the words and then burst into a torrent of tears. I offered her a tissue and waited until she was able to explain further. She told me that she had been investigating some physical problems she was having. Medical examinations uncovered the noncancerous but nonetheless life-threatening tumors. Her doctor's only recommendation was surgery, and it would leave her unable to have children.

Mary could save her life, while sacrificing her future. Her fear was almost palpable. I surmised that in Mary's mind her heavenly Father had become as unpredictable as her own natural father. "How could God let this happen to me?" she asked. She had done everything "perfectly" the last twelve months. Now her newfound security had been undermined. She asked me what I thought she should do.

I was stumped. She had only ten days before the scheduled surgery. Sure, I would pray for her healing, but I sensed that there was an approach I should take that would stabilize her walk in Christ and then help her secure the physical victory of health. Further, I did not want to be presumptuous—demanding that God perform on my timetable.

I instructed Mary to fight her battle with fear first. Then we would pray for her healing with fervor. I told her a story of an elderly woman who had used praise to break the power of fear. Mary liked the method. Over the next seven days she would sing her favorite praise song whenever she started to feel afraid. If necessary, she would excuse herself from the room and find a quiet place. A bathroom or back porch would become her sanctuary. Armed with Isaiah's prophetic statement— "You will keep him in perfect peace, whose mind is stayed on You, because he trusts in You" (Isaiah 26:3, NKJV)—she started the week with great expectations.

At the end of the seven-day period, I walked into my office to see the *old* Mary. She sat smiling and full of joy. She had learned that praise is the language of faith. Later that evening she joined me at a church-wide prayer meeting. Near the end of the prayer service, we called Mary forward. Everyone joined in prayer about the tumors and commanded them to dissolve. Three days later at a pre-surgery examination, the surgeon could not find the tumors. They had shrunk! They were gone. The surgery was cancelled, and Mary was free to live her dream.

Mary's story shows that some problems need strategic prayer. If we can attack the root issue with authoritative prayer, we will have many victories. In fact, I would go so far as to say that sometimes our needs are not as complicated as they look.

The problem is often that far too many of us give lip service to prayer without understanding its discipline or its art. Yet, at the same time, we are seeing a fresh interest in prayer emerge in the Church today. Many more people than ever before are becoming interested in techniques for effective prayer.

This chapter will explain how to cooperate with the Lord in order to pray with authority. Specifically, one of David's psalms will be used to underscore a lifestyle of effective prayer and intercession.

David understood both the external power released in prayer and the personal growth that can come from prayer. The unique insights that God gave him became a power base for his incredible spiritual discernment. Most scholars agree that David gives us a picture of how the Person of the Holy Spirit operates in the life of the believer. With this in mind we can view his life as a prophetic statement about the prayer life of the warrior. We get further insight from the fact that David moved in the threefold anointing of Jesus—prophet, priest and king. As a prophet, David saw into the future and spoke of realities that would be relevant years into the future. As a priest, David worshiped in a manner that brought him into the manifest presence of God. As a king, David learned how to use earthly authority. He got things done in the name of the Lord.

This chapter will end by taking a fresh look at the Lord's Prayer—it can become a springboard to incredible spiritual effectiveness.

"On Display" for a Purpose

Mary's story at the beginning of this chapter reminds us that hopeless situations are opportunities for God to show forth His glory. In the New Testament, Paul suggested that God had put him and other apostles in precarious positions in order to showcase His power. Paul eloquently explained his theory of war this way: "It seems to me that God has put us apostles on display at the end of the procession, like men condemned to die in the arena. We have been made a spectacle to the whole universe, to angels as well as to men" (1 Corinthians 4:9).

The word *spectacle* is the Greek word *theatron*. This word obviously comes from the same root as our word for *theater*. Linguists tell us that this word not only implies the sense of being "put on stage" but also conveys a sense of being made fun of or ridiculed. God, in His infinite wisdom, knows how to confound the wisdom of the wise (see 1 Corinthians 1:19 and Isaiah 29:14). He sets us up in a theater of conflict—or, we might say, sends us into battle—and then rescues us in a way that vindicates His name while drawing men and women to Himself. Mary's story, for instance, has brought many people closer to God.

Spiritual warriors throughout history have learned to trust His goodness in the darkness and heat of battle. Look at the great people of faith in the Bible. Most of them were placed on God-ordained fronts in order to advance the work of God. This happened with Paul repeatedly. No wonder he felt like a spectacle! Look, for instance, at this sequence of events. In Macedonia (see Acts 16), Paul was thrown into jail. Praise and worship at midnight unlocked a door in the spirit realm that allowed the physical doors to be unlocked. In his next stop, Thessalonica, a mob formed in the city and began to riot. You can hear in their shouts the ongoing conflict that faced Paul almost everywhere he went: "These men who have caused trouble all over the world have now come here" (Acts 17:6).

Next, Paul left Thessalonica and ran to Berea. He had great success in the early days but then his old enemies showed up and agitated crowds there, too (see Acts 17:13). Moving on, Paul fled Berea for Athens, where he was persecuted spiritually (see Acts 17:16). He responded by preaching faithfully about their "unknown" God. Shortly thereafter, Paul preached in Corinth (see Acts 18). Given his history of persecution and conflict, Paul must have been greatly encouraged when the Lord appeared to him in a night vision and said the following:

"Do not be afraid; keep on speaking, do not be silent. For I am with you, and no one is going to attack and harm you, because I have many people in this city." So Paul stayed for a year and a half, teaching them the word of God.

Acts 18:9–11

I have just walked you quickly through Paul's journeys through five important cities. These visits were similar to a military campaign: God used this great apostle to move the Gospel through southern Europe. Even though the weapons of his warfare were not fleshly (see 2 Corinthians 10:4), Satan's counterattacks were manifested through specific, organized physical opposition.

In a figurative sense, Paul "attacked the enemy lines" with his entrance into each city. He offered spiritual understanding and salvation to the people in town after town. His strategy was essentially the same in each place. He preached to the Jewish people in the region first, and after that he presented the Gospel to the Gentiles. Throughout this progression, God repeatedly set up a situation in which Paul was put on display (made a spectacle) through conflict. The particular battles differed in each city but the concept was the same everywhere.

Eventually, God's strategy won. Paul was actually successful in planting churches in these regions. Without an understanding of the big picture and willingness to be put "on display," Paul might have easily become distracted or discouraged and ultimately ineffective in carrying out the will of God.

Going back to our story about young Mary, let's remember that her physical test became a setup for her to have a testimony. For all of us, our battles give us an opportunity to show someone the reality of Christ. Paul's teaching was based on both the Scriptures and his experience. When the spotlight of conflict or trouble is upon us, we are in line for divine assistance or intervention. Miracles and breakthroughs can occur in these dark times. In other words, during our "fifteen minutes of fame," speaking in the world's theatrical terms, we can look joyfully for God's glory to be made manifest.

When God chooses to put us on display, we can be sure that He has a plan and a purpose. But suppose we cause our own folly? What if sin leads us to battles that the Lord never meant for us to enter? David shows us two key elements for victory, whether we are in a predicament because of our own bad choices or not. This is the next step in strengthening our power base as prayer warriors.

How to Walk Out of a Mess

David understood exactly how this concept works—this concept of seeing trials as opportunities for victory, and he saw it work in a variety of circumstances. David's life was full of incongruity and puzzling events, yet overall his life was a beautiful symphony in the ears of God. David, the Lord's ultimate warrior, gives us several pointers about how to walk out the lofty concepts we are considering. My favorite psalm, Psalm 3, is the perfect place to start. Let's learn from David's mastery of one of his most difficult trials. This psalm has the heading: "A psalm of David. When he fled from his son Absalom."

> O LORD, how many are my foes! How many rise up against me! Many are saying of me, "God will not deliver him." *Selah*
> But you are a shield around me, O LORD; you bestow glory on me and lift up my head. To the LORD I cry aloud, and he answers me from his holy hill. *Selah*

I lie down and sleep; I wake again, because the LORD sustains me. I will not fear the tens of thousands drawn up against me on every side. Arise, O LORD! Deliver me, O my God! Strike all my enemies on the jaw; break the teeth of the wicked. From the LORD comes deliverance. May your blessing be on your people. *Selah*

Psalm 3:1–8

Let me give you some background. When David described his problem in the first two verses, he said that his foes were many and that they taunted him with refrains that God would not help him. David was referring to Absalom, his son, who had created a civil war by organizing an army against him. As I have mentioned, David had fundamental confusion about developing a godly family. The first place David erred was that he married six women. The children from these marriages were in competition with each other, vying for position. David's home life was in serious trouble. He was an emotionally absent father. This blind spot in David's life gave Satan a place to attack his life and mission.

Absalom had murdered his half brother, Amnon, because Amnon had raped Tamar, Absalom's half sister. David was unable to muster the discipline necessary to bring a sense of order to his home. The kids, therefore, defended themselves on their own terms. So at the root of this civil war was a family problem that had spilled over to his job: His leadership of the government of Israel was in serious jeopardy.

Absalom had turned a great number of people against his father, including some of David's most valued counselors and staff. Thus, when David said, "Many are they who rise up against me," he was telling the truth. Like many of us, David may have wanted to give up in the face of so many problems and such overwhelming pressure.

Yet, even though David was responsible for the doorway through which his problems entered his life, God would rescue him and fulfill His own greater purposes simultaneously.

David had so many problems that he must have asked the question, "Where do I begin?" The answer is revealed in verse 3. David said this: "But thou, O LORD, art a shield for me; my glory, and the lifter up of mine head" (KJV).

Let me explain what this verse means in practical terms. Two things are emphasized here that can be keys to helping you and me get out of our problems. First, when David says *my glory*, he is using this as a term of endearment for the Lord Himself. He is saying that God is his best friend and that in the midst of his problems he is going to focus on praising and bringing glory to God. Second, David understood that the way out of complex problems is to find God's priority list and timing.

Jesus said it this way: "Seek ye first the kingdom of God, and his righteousness; and all these things shall be added unto you" (Matthew 6:33, KJV). In other words, if you seek God's glory first, God will take care of other issues. You do not know what to tackle in the midst of many problems unless God gives you the priorities. You and I cannot fix everything today. What we can do is walk with God, addressing the priorities presented to us. Tackling things this way, God will give us peace on the journey.

Remember our earlier story, when, in the middle of Mary's health problems, the Lord had her deal with a major life-dominating problem—fear? As she learned to praise God in spite of her circumstances, she overcame her fear. This enabled her to take the next step and seek prayer for healing. Not only did she gain a new view of her heavenly Father, but she also received an answer to her prayers—and she continues to bring honor to His name with her powerful testimony. The domino effect that comes from tackling problems in God's ordained sequence releases lasting victory.

As you pray about getting out of your "mess"—whether it is of your own making or not—you will need to give prayerful consideration to prioritizing certain things over others. God will begin to move on your behalf according to His priority. Have you ever prayed about something and wondered why God did not address it? Did it seem odd that you were strangely directed to another issue? If so, it is likely that you did not experience peace until you addressed the issues as presented. This peace may be baffling in light of your problems, but that is because we fail so often to understand God's working in our lives.

Our tendency is to focus on things we cannot control or change, while God often wants us to deal with the problems we can control. Our motives, our attitudes, restoring broken relationships, taking responsibility are all things we can do. In light of this, some of our agenda items need to be put on "pause." This does not mean that we don't deal with our problems; it just means that we must trust God's direction.

Returning to Psalm 3, remember David said that God was "my glory and the lifter of my head." After finding God's priorities in the midst of our problems, we find God's power coming behind us. The phrase *lifter of my head* is a Hebrew term used for God being our victor, one who defeats our enemies. When our heads are bowed down in shame, pressure and defeat, He lifts us and delivers us out of our problems.

Let me give you an example. Suppose you sense God telling you this: *I know you are having problems on your job, but right now the most important thing for you to deal with is your relationship with your oldest child.* What you do is press the "pause" button on the concern about your job issues. Naturally, you give your best at your job and endure the pressure, but you address first the problems God directs you to. This will lead to a victory with the child. Then God will lift your head up in the job situation as well.

God has a way of making it clear to us what His priorities are. When He tells us His agenda, there is often a "disconnect" between our concepts and God's guidance. We may feel confused. Be careful about this. Many people say they are confused about the will of God, when really they just do not agree. These people are in rebellion.

Note that in all of these trials and conflicts and battles, God is in control. This means that He will answer all of your prayers—but He might not answer all of them the way you want. This is why a foundation of praise is critical before you tackle the priorities He sets before you. Praise brings you to the place of trust. As you move in trust, you find that you can manage your expectations and energy. Then, whatever the particular outcome, you have the assurance that He will work everything together for your ultimate good.

A "Training" Prayer

Famed devotional writer E. M. Bounds made an important statement about the nature of prayer and how to pursue it effectively. He said:

> The goal of prayer is the ear of God, a goal that can only be reached by patient and continued and continuous waiting upon Him, pouring out our heart to Him and permitting Him to speak to us. Only by so doing can we expect to know Him, and as we come to know Him better

we shall spend more time in His presence and find that presence a constant and ever-increasing delight.[1]

The Lord's Prayer is one of the best training documents to help us enter into the realm of effective prayer Bounds is talking about. We have sometimes made this prayer overly complicated. Jesus was a master teacher with the ability to take complex subjects and boil them down to the epitome of simplicity.

Look at Matthew 6:9–15:

> "This, then, is how you should pray: 'Our Father in heaven, hallowed be your name, your kingdom come, your will be done on earth as it is in heaven. Give us today our daily bread. Forgive us our debts, as we also have forgiven our debtors. And lead us not into temptation, but deliver us from the evil one.' For if you forgive men when they sin against you, your heavenly Father will also forgive you. But if you do not forgive men their sins, your Father will not forgive your sins."

This particular passage of Scripture is the highest revelation of prayer we have in the New Testament. In it we find three points that the Lord sets as the foundation for our prayers. We should pray for:

- Our daily bread
- Forgiveness of people who have hurt us
- Guidance away from personal temptation

With these three specific prayer points to focus upon, we can keep ourselves on track. In the Lord's Prayer, we are given permission to discuss our struggles freely and openly. We need not worry about money or become emotionally congested by a lack of forgiveness. The third point of this prayer platform is perhaps the most important. The phrase *deliver us from evil* is really saying, "Rescue us, protect us from all evil things!" Humanly speaking, the evil things that hinder us are both external and internal in origin. Thankfully, God has a wonderful plan for each of our lives. Sometimes in our hurry to do things for God and family, we rush ahead of the Lord and create problems instead of seizing opportunities. Satan's goal is to create a deceptive strategy that will cause us to fall short of the Lord's lofty calling.

As I am writing these words, I am sitting in the comfort of my home in a "secret" place that I use to reflect, pray and exercise. This is my domain in the house. It is a "guy room." Decorated sparsely, it reflects a Spartan discipline that I hope to recapture in my life. In this environment, I can evaluate my thoughts, words and deeds honestly. As recently as yesterday, my prayer time here led me to put these prayer points into action. I did so, last night, when I had a discussion with an old friend, someone who has helped launch our ministry into important dimensions. In fact, this woman has been one of my greatest supporters.

Yesterday I realized that I had inadvertently offended this woman. I made a brash decision and took some unwise steps. Every day some of the worst problems in my life are the result of my clumsy navigation of unfamiliar territory. My intentions, from my perspective, are noble. Despite my lofty goals, I often feel like a man at a formal gathering who comes strolling out of the bathroom with toilet paper stuck to his shoes. My desires and motives are mixed. I sometimes talk about God's glory, while pursuing my own personal gain.

I prayed the three specific prayer points from the Lord's Prayer, repenting for my mistakes, and suddenly a clear direction emerged for mending the breach I had caused in our relationship.

Perhaps the best way to explain what happens in prayer is to repeat the words of Major-General Orde Wingate:

> Finally, knowing the vanities of man's efforts and the confusion of his purpose, let us pray that God may accept our services and direct our endeavours, so that when we shall have done all we shall see the fruits of our labours and be satisfied.[2]

I thank God that He is helping me get delivered from myself—my old habits, my shortsightedness and my selfishness. All of us can choose to grow to become powerful warriors for the King and the Kingdom. It starts when we decide that we will be willing to enter whatever theater God chooses for us. It continues as we develop an attitude of praise. And it culminates in letting God direct our steps and entrusting the outcome to Him.

Now we are ready to go to the next chapter and discuss our outlook or attitudes. Let's take a moment first, though, to assimilate what we have already learned about praying in authority.

TAKING INVENTORY

1. Like Mary in the opening story, have you ever entertained dreams that crashed into an abyss of reality?
2. Have you ever used praise as a focus instead of fear? Why does this change of focus help?
3. What is "perfect peace" (Isaiah 26:3)? How do we obtain it?
4. Looking at the European tour Paul made, do you see parallels to situations you face in your life?

Through Paul's example, do you see keys to your situations that will make you a "spectacle" on display for God's glory?

5. Personalize Psalm 3 to your life in the following aspects:
   - Who are your foes?
   - What do people say about you?
   - Where do you see God's shield about you?
   - How is God answering you from His holy hill?
   - How is God currently sustaining you?
   - Are you overcoming your fears in a particular area?
   - Where do you need God's deliverance?
   - Where do you need His blessing?

6. Take time to pray the three principles from the Lord's Prayer: asking for your daily bread, seeking forgiveness of people who have hurt you (or restitution with someone you have hurt) and receiving guidance away from personal temptation.

8

Outlook

The Ultimate Secret Weapon

I have often thought that the best way to define a man's character would be to seek out the particular mental or moral attitude in which, when it came upon him, he felt himself most deeply and intensely active and alive. At such moments there is a voice inside which speaks and says: "This is the real me!"

William James

In January 2004, an amazing phenomenon occurred. One of the most successful coaches of all time returned to football at the ripe young age of 63 years. Having taken a break of eleven years, he proved the new adage that says that fifty is the new thirty. Statisticians tell us that workers entering the marketplace today may have as many as five different career transitions in their lifetimes.

Joe Gibbs has navigated his transitions more adeptly than most. Professional sports at any level are very lucrative but highly competitive. Gibbs set the bar for performance in his chosen field. His record is the fourteenth best in NFL history: 140 wins. He did this in only twelve years. Other coaches recording more wins than Gibbs did so with at least four more seasons under their belts. His overall winning percentage for those years was nearly 70 percent.

As head coach of the Washington Redskins, he won three Super Bowls with three different quarterbacks. He was named to the Pro Football Hall of Fame in Canton, Ohio, in 1996.

Gibbs was known to be thorough, hardworking and fully engaged in his job. His Christian character was also widely known and respected as one of his strengths. His integrity teamed with his skill to yield great success.

Yet Gibbs, like the rest of us, wrestled with personal problems. It is interesting how virtue or blemishes in our character help define our unique personal fingerprints and the marks we leave in history. In Gibbs' case, the "tragic flaw"—as poetic writers often call it—almost destroyed his terrific testimony. In his biography, *Racing to Win: Establish Your Game Plan for Success*, the coach opened up. He explained his struggle, and his eventual victory.

What was the problem? On three occasions during his early football career, Gibbs fell prey to financial temptation. Mixed motives and bad business deals produced a mountain of debt that weighed heavily upon him and his family. The enemy had made a major inroad into his life. Gibbs admits that privately he displayed bravado concerning business dealings. Perhaps pride in the financial arena kept him from seeking both expert advice and God. And equally undermining was a fundamental lack of trust in God's ability to provide for him if and when he had to leave football. Anxiety about his future gnawed at him. The fear of loss may have been so deafening that he could not hear any other voice.

It was the third financial temptation that became Gibbs' biggest problem. With a consortium of business partners, he invested in a huge real-estate development project. Millions of dollars of debt stacked up. After contemplating bankruptcy, Gibbs prayerfully decided to apply the Bible's teaching on character to his life. He repented of his sin and of ignoring his wife's suggestions and warnings. He began to change his outlook or attitude about success and finances. He began to thirst after righteousness and pure motives. "It took more than four and a half years of hard work, sacrifice, and commitment, but inch by inch, our family walked out from under the dark financial cloud that had enveloped us,"[1] writes Gibbs.

Advancing Christ's agenda in our lives will take spiritual responses that are not necessarily "natural" to us personally. At the height of Gibbs' career, just after he had whipped his personal demons, he resigned from football. His reasons for retiring were twofold. First, he wanted to spend more time with his family. Second, he wanted to address some health problems.

Free from the fear of financial insecurity, Gibbs was able to pursue the will of God for himself and his family. Ironically, after eleven years of work in other areas, in which he also found amazing success, he has returned to his beloved football. After Gibbs placed his "Isaac" (football) on an altar of sacrifice, the Lord has chosen to guide the coach back into the game.

Dr. Robert Clinton, author of a landmark book entitled *The Making of a Leader* (NavPress, 1988), might say that Coach Gibbs has entered the "convergence phase" of his life. Convergence is a season of life in which all our major strengths come together—spiritual lessons, natural gifts, training, personal passion and influence for Christ. If Gibbs is in the convergence phase of his life, as I suggest, the coach will see his greatest years of victory and witness for Christ in the years ahead.

The Lord often waits to release our greatest influence or potential until we have been "checked out" from every angle, until our motives have been purged and our attitudes aligned with Christ's agenda. In this chapter we will examine the outlook or attitudes that we as Christian warriors must have to advance the cause of Christ in the correct spirit. The teachings of Christ known as the Beatitudes will be the foundation of our study. We will see, as well, that David understood some of these Holy Spirit–inspired concepts.

Jesus promised that people who possess eight counter-cultural attitudes or experiences would be truly blessed by God Himself. And He was not referring just to external blessings; people who embrace this teaching are also promised inner peace, fulfillment and happiness. You may recall that Robert H. Schuller wrote a book on this subject with the memorable title *The Be (Happy) Attitudes*.

The Beatitudes are popular in concept but quite unpopular when it comes to applying them personally in our lives. They are almost the opposite of the world's way of doing things. We cannot ignore the fact, however, that our attitudes inspire our actions—a vital concept for our training as warriors. Why are these something of a secret weapon for us? Because Jesus declared that people who develop these eight attitudes will be especially noticed by God. A unique dimension of favor will be released into the lives of those who harbor these attitudes instead of bitterness, envy, resentment or other negative mental perspectives. He said that the following people are blessed:

- The poor in spirit
- Those who mourn
- The meek
- Those who hunger and thirst for righteousness
- The merciful
- The pure at heart
- The peacemakers
- Those persecuted because of righteousness

If we embrace these aspects of the Beatitudes, we can turn our world on its ear! Let's look at them briefly one by one.

The Poor in Spirit

"Blessed are the poor in spirit, for theirs is the kingdom of heaven" (Matthew 5:3).

There are two different Greek words for *poor*. One speaks of the working poor. The other describes the abject poor—those who have nothing at all. Surprisingly, the word used in this passage is the word for abject poverty. Jesus is saying that the man who is desperately poor is actually blessed. True happiness lies in understanding our utter depravity before God and our complete need for Him.

The poor in spirit are those who realize that they have no ability in themselves to please God. They consciously depend on God, therefore, not on themselves.

Jesus says essentially that material wealth or recognition of our ability can work against true spirituality. Paul says it this way: "When I am weak, then I am strong" (2 Corinthians 12:10). He taught unequivocally that having a dependent spirit always caused the power of the Holy Spirit to rest upon him.

Let's take a moment to apply this truth. When a person thinks, like the young Joe Gibbs, *I can take care of myself*, the Lord often backs away. Contrary to normal human thinking, weakness and poverty of spirit attract the grace of God. Trying to produce human bravado instead of the confidence of faith does not impress God. Understanding this concept about the poor in spirit, David said, "This poor man called, and the LORD heard him; he saved him out of all his troubles. The angel of the LORD encamps around those who fear him, and he delivers them" (Psalm 34:6–7).

This psalm was a part of David's training of four hundred men at the caves of Adullam, men who came to him in debt, distressed and discouraged. David built upon the understanding of being "poor in spirit" and other truths to turn these men into true warriors for God.

Those Who Mourn

"Blessed are those who mourn, for they will be comforted" (Matthew 5:4).

True compassion will lead us to a sense of mourning. And mourning that identifies with the Lord's agenda will release His power. This does not apply just to our own concerns; there is a blessing attached when we join in mourning about the state of affairs of people around us. The Scriptures record the phrase *Jesus was moved with compassion* five times. After each of these statements, Jesus performed a miracle of healing or provision.

Spiritual warriors must learn to have deep inner peace while allowing their hearts to abide in "the house of mourning." King Solomon coined this phrase and it describes the attitude that the truly wise must maintain, without becoming cynical or jaded. Solomon's words in the book of Ecclesiastes are as follows:

The heart of the wise is in the house of mourning; but the heart of fools is in the house of mirth. It is better to hear the rebuke of the wise, than for a man to hear the song of fools. For as the crackling of thorns under a pot, so is the laughter of the fool: this also is vanity.

Ecclesiastes 7:4–6, KJV

The Meek

"Blessed are the meek, for they will inherit the earth" (Matthew 5:5).

In our 21st-century parlance, meekness does not sound flattering at all. It implies weakness. It may even go as far as to imply a cowardly, easily influenced individual. The Greek word for *meek* is the word *praus*, suggesting strong ethics. To be meek meant to be strong, controlled and disciplined. Years ago, I heard a famous scholar comparing meekness to a championship horse that was under bit and bridle. He suggested that meekness is a description of strength under direction.

Scottish New Testament scholar William Barclay translates this verse as: "Blessed is the man who is always angry at the right time, and never angry at the wrong time."[2]

This paraphrase of Jesus' words in the Greek cultural context shows strength of conviction and personal control. This strength is not initiated by human standards alone. Through the prophet Isaiah, the Lord described a person He esteems as someone "who is humble and contrite in spirit, and trembles at my word" (Isaiah 66:2).

David addressed the rewards of meekness. His concept of meekness adds a measure of humility to the definitions we have given already. This warring king considered a meek man as someone who would humbly take to heart the commandments of God, obey them in fear and trembling, and control his temper in the heat of battle.

Hear are three passages of Scripture to meditate upon in this regard:

> "The meek shall eat and be satisfied: they shall praise the LORD that seek him: your heart shall live for ever" (Psalm 22:26, KJV).

> "Good and upright is the LORD: therefore will he teach sinners in the way. The meek will he guide in judgment: and the meek will he teach his way" (Psalm 25:8–9, KJV).

> "For yet a little while, and the wicked shall not be: yea, thou shalt diligently consider his place, and it shall not be. But the meek shall inherit the earth; and shall delight themselves in the abundance of peace" (Psalm 37:10–11, KJV).

Those Who Hunger and Thirst for Righteousness

"Blessed are those who hunger and thirst for righteousness, for they will be filled" (Matthew 5:6).

Of the attitudes discussed thus far, this beatitude has the most obvious meaning. There is only one aspect of this verse that is less obvious.

Consider the kind of hunger that we might have for a meal. If I am extremely famished, I will eat until I am filled. Linguistic scholars suggest, however, that this verse describes a different kind of hunger; it reflects a complete state of righteousness. The dinner image, then, would be that I eat until everything is gone. This is very different from eating until I am full. People who desire a little truth, righteousness and justice are easy to find.

The number of people who long to learn, understand and obey *everything* the Lord requires are few. These people want to eat the whole loaf of bread instead of simply filling their stomachs. They want to eat all the food in the restaurant instead of stopping at dessert.

David also knew something about spiritual hunger. Having touched the richness of the Lord's presence, he longed for intimacy with God that would transform his character. Listen to words from David's song of hunger for righteousness:

> O God, you are my God, earnestly I seek you; my soul thirsts for you, my body longs for you, in a dry and weary land where there is no water. I have seen you in the sanctuary and beheld your power and your glory. Because your love is better than life, my lips will glorify you. I will praise you as long as I live, and in your name I will lift up my hands. My soul will be satisfied as with the richest of foods; with singing lips my mouth will praise you.
>
> Psalm 63:1–5

The Merciful

"Blessed are the merciful, for they will be shown mercy" (Matthew 5:7).

This, again, is a simple concept. The Lord wants every believer to sow mercy as a seed. As we give mercy to others, we will receive the same from the Lord. The apostle James gives a stern warning to legalistic believers who, like the Prodigal Son's elder brother in Luke 15, do not rejoice when God shows mercy to wayward people. James states clearly: "Speak and act as those who are going to be judged by the law that gives freedom, because judgment without mercy will be shown to anyone who has not been merciful. Mercy triumphs over judgment!" (James 2:12–13).

For years I wondered how David got away with the many sins he committed. The Lord even went so far as to say that David was a man after his own heart (see Acts 13:22). In human thinking it is difficult to reconcile the heinous, deceptive murder of Uriah with God's compliments about the life of David. It seems that God truly blots out sin. David attributed his longevity and strength to God's covenant with the merciful.

Let me give you an example of David's kindness before we take a look at his teachings for the generations that would follow him. After all that David had endured at the hands of Saul, he could easily have rejoiced that Saul and his sons were dead and the throne was finally his. He did not do so. Instead, he asked the question, "Is there yet any that is left of the house of Saul, that I may show him kindness for Jonathan's sake?" (2 Samuel 9:1, KJV). David found out about a young, crippled man named Mephibosheth, who had been lame since he was five years old. He was Saul's grandson and Jonathan's son. David sent for this man and his young son and fed them both at his table. This act of kindness shows the merciful heart of David.

A few years later, David was betrayed by his son Absalom and wound up showing mercy to Mephibosheth again. David's kindness to the downtrodden may be why he survived so many battles, betrayals and wars, both great and small.

Please meditate on Psalm 37:24–26 and ask God to open your eyes to see how to apply this principle:

> Though he fall, he shall not be utterly cast down: for the LORD upholdeth him with his hand. I have been young, and now am old; yet have I not seen the righteous for-

saken, nor his seed begging bread. He is ever merciful, and lendeth; and his seed is blessed."

KJV

The Pure in Heart

"Blessed are the pure in heart, for they will see God" (Matthew 5:8).

One of the great intricacies within Christianity is that our motivations are judged, not simply our actions. If a man lusts after a woman in his heart, it is sin. The apostle James explains the reasoning for this by saying that thoughts give birth to mindsets, and mindsets give birth to deeds (see James 1:13–15). Thus, if I sin with my mind, my body will eventually get involved. It is just a matter of time. On the flip side, if I meditate on the Word of God and Christian testimonies and teachings, I will be prompted to act in keeping with the focus of my thought life.

David articulates how this works:

> The LORD has rewarded me according to my righteousness, according to the cleanness of my hands in his sight. To the faithful you show yourself faithful, to the blameless you show yourself blameless, to the pure you show yourself pure, but to the crooked you show yourself shrewd. You save the humble but bring low those whose eyes are haughty. You, O LORD, keep my lamp burning; my God turns my darkness into light.

Psalm 18:24–28

The Peacemakers

"Blessed are the peacemakers, for they will be called sons of God" (Matthew 5:9).

The Greek word for *peace* is *eirene*. It is similar in meaning to the Hebrew word for peace—*shalom*. It is a positive word, speaking of completeness, soundness, welfare.[3] Interestingly, the Hebrew word for *peace* is very similar to the word for prosperity. True peacemakers desire the best for the people they serve.

A great way to illustrate this is to tell you a true story that happened to me. I drove up to my favorite hotel a few months ago just in time to see two men yelling at each other. I realized that I recognized one of the men. I watched amazed as one of them swung a fist at the other. The response was a karate-like kick. I found myself yelling at them to stop. Then I jumped out of my car and forced myself between the two men, who finally gave up the fight. Then I lectured the man whom I knew concerning his behavior. I told him that he could have been hurt in that fight. Since I knew something of him personally, I also warned him that he could have lost his job if he had persisted in the violence.

Then I turned and walked into the beautiful lobby. It was only as I reached the front desk that I realized that I could have been hurt. One of them could have pulled a weapon on me. Policemen have found far too often that sometimes both angry parties turn on the peacemaker. What was I thinking?

I was thinking of the welfare of the two men. My concern for them caused me to forget about myself. I realized that being a peacemaker does not mean that we always walk into peaceful situations; it may mean quite the opposite. In fact, a peace lover may not be brave enough to become a peacemaker.

In Matthew 10:11–13, the Lord instructed His disciples to go into cities and into specific houses looking for people who wanted the inner peace that they could give. Jesus told His disciples to let their peace literally come upon the houses of those who were searching for peace. The blessing of being a peacemaker means that we carry grace from God to introduce people to the Prince of Peace. This usually means personal contact, but we can also create an atmosphere of personal peace in someone's life through our prayers.

Notice Jesus said that peacemakers would be called sons of God. The trickiest aspect of this verse is that the word translated as "sons" is the Greek word *huios*. It refers to a mature son. First of all, only mature sons can apply the relational skills that bring the peace of God into complex situations. Second, strong Christians should be willing to be used by the Lord to bring His glory into difficult circumstances. In other words, the Lord delights in sending mature Christians into progressively chaotic situations in order to bring people to a place of illumination, salvation and peace.

David's war experience had already taught him that courage sometimes requires action. Long before the teachings of Christ, David lived under the blessings of being a peacekeeper and someone who sought the order of God in his nation.

Those Persecuted because of Righteousness

"Blessed are those who are persecuted because of righteousness, for theirs is the kingdom of heaven" (Matthew 5:10).

Last but not least, this beatitude reminds us that our Christian walk is not just about our convenience. Many of David's psalms seem to revolve around how badly he was treated by his adversaries. Persecution is part of a powerful Christian walk. Jesus described the reward of suffering through persecution as follows:

"I tell you the truth," Jesus replied, "no one who has left home or brothers or sisters or mother or father or children or fields for me and the gospel will fail to receive a hundred times as much in this present age (homes, brothers, sisters, mothers, children and fields—and with them, persecutions) and in the age to come, eternal life."

Mark 10:29–30

In Principle

Our outlook and attitudes about life determine how much we will accomplish. One of the most effective military leaders of all time, Napoleon Bonaparte, made this observation about life: "Get your principles straight; the rest is a matter of details."[4]

Living a principled life gives a person a sense of direction and a way to measure success. Principles help keep us on a specific path. Abraham Lincoln lived by the code of honesty more strictly than most. This informed observation of his has helped me a great deal: "I am not bound to win, but I am bound to be true. I am not bound to succeed, but I am bound to live up to what light I have."[5]

Take a moment now to think about truth, light and your calling to maintain a godly outlook and attitude.

TAKING INVENTORY

1. Do you identify with the story of Joe Gibbs in terms of mistakes that you have made? Did they seem too overwhelming to recover from? Have you ever felt that God told you to do something that seemed

illogical or perhaps mistimed but through your obedience, you were rewarded?

2. Meditate on the Beatitudes as they apply to your life today. What have you learned that can make a difference in how you apply the principles that Jesus taught?
   - The poor in spirit
   - Those who mourn
   - The meek
   - Those who hunger and thirst for righteousness
   - The merciful
   - The pure in heart
   - The peacemakers
   - Those persecuted because of righteousness

3. What truth have you gained by this study of attitudes that can be woven into your daily life immediately?

4. Has God shed any light on dark or hidden areas that need to be addressed? Take time to confess any shortcomings and ask the Holy Spirit to guide you into newness.

9

Reconciliation

Balm for the Wounded

Men with clenched fists cannot shake hands.

Anonymous

The movie was great—full of action! You know, the kind
with horses galloping, guns blazing and the tall, hand-
some hero vanquishing the "bad guys" to save the day.
Guy stuff all the way! The handful of love scenes was
tolerable for a twelve-year-old raised in the sixties. A
late bloomer, I had not yet discovered girls. As Dad and
I laughed about various scenes, I suddenly asked an
unexpected question: "Why were those people trying to
hurt the only black man in the movie? Why were they
so cruel to him just because he was black?"

I just didn't understand. Perhaps I was becoming
conscious of this issue because I had recently begun

attending a previously all-white prep school. There were only two of us black kids in the seventh grade. Reggie Garrett was the other African-American, one of the smartest kids I had ever met. Later in high school he scored 1600 on the SATs.

As Dad and I walked and talked, I reflected on my personal racial history, I found it pretty uneventful. My earliest memories were fairly innocuous. Oh, there was the time that the Western movie star I loved came to town. I was only about seven years old. I begged my mother to take me to see him. Let's call him "Mr. Big West." After standing in line for hours waiting my turn, I finally stepped forward to get his autograph, but Mr. Big West just spun around and walked away. My mom, whom I never heard curse in my whole life, came the closest to using some "choice" words at that moment.

I wasn't hurt by the rejection. I was just confused. This was my hero. Episode after episode, Mr. Big West always did the right thing and said the right words. *Maybe he is tired*, I thought. Mom and I rode home in silence and never talked about the incident again.

When the civil rights movement hit its stride, it came as a shock to me. Perhaps this was because the school, stores, church and neighborhood of my world were black. There were no separate bathrooms for blacks where I lived. The "back of the bus" was also a foreign concept to me. People in our city got along for the most part.

About the same time, I remember the Black Muslims coming to our door and handing out their newspapers. My dad would always tell us, "Be nice to them . . . but don't listen to anything they have to say."

Later, I experienced the riots in Cincinnati. It was a scary time. Militant blacks threw bricks through the car windows of innocent whites just for driving through our neighborhood. Then the National Guard was sent out to our community. One day I stepped out on the porch to get some air, and six or seven jeeps swooshed past me. Suddenly, all of their guns were pointed back at me. It was an eerie feeling. I could have been shot on the porch of my own house.

Let's go back to my post-movie discussion with my dad. My father's face took on a strange glow as he talked to me about racism. For him racism was a mental disease. He explained that the first person to see his academic potential was a white fellow whom he worked for part time. He challenged me to give the white kids a chance to really prove their friendship. My father reminded me that his grandfather was white and that my grandmother was a full-blooded Cherokee Indian.

The prep school for Cincinnati's privileged that I attended led to amazing choices for college. Williams College and Harvard University were the choices I made for undergraduate and graduate schools, respectively. The chance discussion with my father about seeing people as individuals rather than stereotypes had changed my life.

Fast-forwarding to the spring of 1981, six of us started a prayer meeting with two black couples and one white couple. Our little town was the northern most tip of Appalachia. This semirural area was also the home of a major Fortune 500 company. Poverty met privilege in this amazing little place. Ph.D.s walked downtown with farmers, and engineers had close friendships with factory workers. Prestige was understated and the common man was treated with kindness. It seemed as though the past, present and future flowed together without competition or disrespect. In summation, Corning, New York, was a delightful place to live.

It was astonishing to me that only 1 percent of the population was black. A small church that I pastored served the needs of the handful of blacks living in that region. But we realized that if we wanted to have a church of more than 25 people, we would have to cross the color barrier. During the next few years, our little church led hundreds of people to Christ. The church eventually became 95 to 97 percent white. It mirrored the racial diversity of the community. In the 1980s this was unheard of. We became one of the first predominately white churches in the country to have a black leader.

Time will not allow me to speak of our methods and approaches that produced unity of vision and purpose. Suffice it to say that we learned how to develop in people the ability to see beyond the flesh. At our core we possessed a belief in the power of Christ's love. The love of God expressed by our members transcended race. It transcended culture. The reality of this love was not based on a doctrine of unity; rather, the love created a bond of unity that was unbreakable.

The training we gave people was based upon David's model in Psalm 34. We did not attempt to teach that pioneer group about racial reconciliation *per se*. Instead we taught the members a worldview that became so big it eclipsed the concepts of class and race that they possessed before they came to our church.

In this chapter we will do two things. First of all, we must develop a proper understanding of where the concept of racial reconciliation came from, for it is the basis of all reconciliation. Second, we will study the principles David taught his men. These principles made them natural reconcilers of men to God.

Reconciling the Church

Racial and cultural reconciliation has become a major buzzword for the Christian world. Over the years, I have been asked by more pastors than I can number how they can integrate their churches. Yet, without learning how to walk in humility and love, lasting racial reconciliation is not really possible.

The quick-fix approach to integrating a church is often based on a new form of political correctness. This politically correct approach attempts to manufacture by marketing or social architecture something that only God Himself can do. Only God can erase cultural and racial hatred from the heart of an individual. Many people try to force the visible manifestation of a racially mixed church before it is God's time to do this.

Overemphasis on racial harmony can forge a church system that promotes tokens. Token black leaders in a predominately white church feel honored upon their appointment, but dishonored when they realize that no one wants to hear their teaching or counsel.

Think about it this way. Imagine someone receiving a kidney transplant. Only the right organ nurtured in the right way will be received by the diseased body of someone in need of a kidney. The Body of Christ has often been guilty of transplanting organs based upon very superficial analysis. The long-term negative result in these cases may be harder to detect in the spiritual body than they are in the natural body. For a few years, structural and organization techniques function like clever surgical procedures to put things in place. But despite our hard work, the body accepts these grafted organs only on its own terms.

An unbalanced focus on racial harmony will have local churches and parachurch ministries cutting out healthy organs and replacing them with diseased ones. Or even worse, we will find ourselves performing life-threatening surgery for purely cosmetic reasons. We must remember that the spiritual Body of Christ is already *one*. It is already unified. Believers have to be taught to celebrate the unity we have in Christ. Once we begin to celebrate the reality of our unity, the Lord can direct us into meaningful affiliations and tasks. The natural body is connected based upon function. Joints, for example, are designed strategically to assist bones and muscles. The spiritual body must also recognize that the point of spiritual unity is not window dressing. It is to serve a higher, divinely inspired purpose.

While in some places Sunday morning is the most segregated hour of the week, in others there is a veritable potpourri of diversity. The essential question mature believers must ask is this: Is this portion of the Body working obediently within the call of God for our lives? Some "mono-racial" churches are flowing wonderfully in the call of God upon their ministry. Others are in subterranean rebellion against God's vision for their corporate mission. The height of human pride is to think that we have to engineer churches to look like what we want by keeping out certain ethnic groups or manipulating others to work as part of our team.

The concept of true racial reconciliation is taken from several passages of Scripture, but Paul's words in 2 Corinthians 5:14–16 are seminal to the argument. Paul's message is as follows:

> For Christ's love compels us, because we are convinced that one died for all, and therefore all died. . . . So from now on we regard no one from a worldly point of view. Though we once regarded Christ in this way, we do so no longer.

The phrase *from now on we regard no one from a worldly point of view* is critical here. Please note that "a worldly point of view" does not refer simply to black and white relationships. A clearheaded analysis of Paul's vision suggests that quirky people with no ethnic defense for their problems need to be loved. Likewise, members of our favorite minority may need compassion and ministry. True love should not be feigned; the Lord must assign each relationship within the Body.

In my years in upstate New York, I learned to love the economically lowly farmers, along with the upwardly mobile junior executives. I discovered that the power of the Holy Spirit is available to birth deep compassion in my life for those that I am called to reach out to in ministry relationships.

True reconcilers are exactly like the peacemakers we discussed in the last chapter. They learn to build bridges with others. Describing this quality in his own life, Paul makes several startling statements. The passage below speaks of the distinctions Paul chose to bridge:

> Though I am free and belong to no man, I make myself a slave to everyone, to win as many as possible. To the Jews I became like a Jew, to win the Jews. To those under the law I became like one under the law (though I myself am not under the law), so as to win those under the law. To those not having the law I became like one not having the law (though I am not free from God's law but am under Christ's law), so as to win those not having the law. To the weak I became weak, to win the weak. I have become all things to all men so that by all possible means I might save some. I do all this for the sake of the gospel, that I may share in its blessings.
>
> 1 Corinthians 9:19–23

Paul lived in the reality and power of the Gospel. He also lived to present the Gospel. Many of his fellow Christians were limited in their ability to connect with different cultural worlds. Thus, Paul knew that he had to develop the ability to size people up and reach them where they were. Because of his desire to win souls, he learned how to find common ground with people he wanted to reach.

First of all, Paul successfully reached people hung up on being culturally Jewish as the primary identity factor of their lives. Second, those with legalistic views of their faith (they try to keep all the rules) were ongoing targets for Paul's teaching in synagogues. Third, he discovered ways to draw in the biblically illiterate who had never understood the Old Testament requirements. Finally, Paul learned how to get past his disgust for people he once judged as being weak.

Understanding the worldview of others is critical to heart communication and connection. The descriptions in the verses above are just a sample of the bridges he typically crossed in preaching, teaching and relationships. In my view, this passage of Scripture was written so that the readers would understand the need to reach the target communities Christ has placed in their lives.

Paul shows us the bridges we want to cross. Let's turn now to David for the tools we need to build them.

Developing Mature Warriors

David was on the run from King Saul when he stopped at a place called Nob. Desperate and hungry, he convinced a priest to give him sacred bread—showbread—for food. Ironically, the priest had somehow also gained possession of the great sword of Goliath. It was the only weapon he had. The priest methodically unwrapped the sword and gave it to the great folk hero.

Fear would not allow David to rest. David's next stop, according to 1 Samuel 21, was in the neighboring kingdom of Gath, Goliath's home region. The sword, of all things, gave David away as the famed giant killer. As the people tried to bring him before the king, David began to act crazy. He started drooling on himself and made marks on the doors of the gate. The king of Gath would not allow David to stay in his presence and sent him away. David then wandered to a place called Adullam, which means "justice to the people."

Adullam was a place with huge caves. Imagine them like various meeting rooms in the largest hotels. Some of the caverns were so huge, it was like having several ballrooms that could seat two or three hundred people. This natural conference center became the training ground for the Lord; He sent large numbers of people to David here. There was only one catch to this assignment—all the men who came to David had problems (see 1 Samuel 22:2). They were distressed, in debt or discontented. Based on their personal histories, they were desperate for change.

David realized that he had to turn this motley group of four hundred men into a crack army. Psalm 34 is a record of the highlights of his teaching. This song combines David's personal testimony with the benefits of living for God. It seems to be a summary of the lessons he learned at the peak of his early walk with God. The psalm describes the five dimensions of training David took men through on their journey to reconciliation with God and man. He took men without strong personal identities and made them champions for God. As they learned about God, they became bridge builders.

The steps are as follows:

- Prayer
- Protection
- Provision
- Positive proclamations
- Probity

Let's look at these one by one.

Grasping the Power of Prayer

I will extol the LORD at all times; his praise will always be on my lips. My soul will boast in the LORD; let the afflicted hear and rejoice. Glorify the LORD with me; let us exalt his name together. I sought the LORD, and he answered me; he delivered me from all my fears.

Psalm 34:1–4

We have already devoted an entire chapter to prayer. Each one of David's disciples had to learn how to move in several kinds of prayer for two important reasons. David taught his men, first, that the invisible realm is more powerful that the natural realm of kings, armies and swords. They had to learn that true strength comes in praising the Lord and extolling His name.

Second, David practiced listening prayer. David admitted in verse 4 that he struggled with numerous fears. The word translated as "sought" is the Hebrew word *darash*. It has the connotation of inquiring of God with the intention of hearing from Him. This is two-way prayer. My sense is that David not only had general confidence in God but also prayed until he knew the Lord's specific will. David seemed to live a lifestyle of prayer when he was in his worst pinches. Interestingly, when David was engaged with external war, he did not seem to have to fight so many of his personal battles.

I say this because David's greatest sins were committed when he let his guard down emotionally. Once, after a season of intense battles, he grew complacent. He had established a terrific administration and the people were receiving justice. Further, the Ammonites and the Syrians were both defeated. David was probably more emotionally exhausted than he realized, so—even though it was a time for war—he decided to stay home and sent Joab, his commander-in-chief to lead the troops. First Chronicles 20:1 says,

> In the spring, at the time when kings go off to war, Joab led out the armed forces. He laid waste the land of the Ammonites and went to Rabbah and besieged it, but David remained in Jerusalem.

The trouble came not long after this episode. We read in 1 Chronicles 21 that David was "incited" by Satan to take a census of Israel. His commanders tried to dissuade him from numbering the soldiers in this manner, probably because it gave the impression of trusting in military might rather than the Lord, but David persisted. This census displeased God greatly and brought punishment on the people of Israel: Seventy thousand men fell dead in a sweeping plague (see 1 Chronicles 21:14).

The lesson to learn here is that we can never take a vacation from a life of prayer and devotion to God.

Living under the Protective Cover of God

> Those who look to him are radiant; their faces are never covered with shame. This poor man called, and the LORD heard him; he saved him out of all his troubles. The angel of the LORD encamps around those who fear him, and he delivers them.
>
> Psalm 34:5–7

David believed that when he or his men lived in a prayer lifestyle they would be covered with God's protection (see also Psalm 27:5). David prayed, but after prayer he took a step that many of us do not take—he rested in God. He believed that Almighty God encamped around him.

David taught his men to do away with groundless shame and self-depreciation. Sometimes we feel shame because we are aware of multiple layers of sin in our lives. This guilt work of sin can be dealt with only through specific personal repentance. Once we are secure in our positions in Christ, we can be secure in the protection of Christ. In fact, the phrase *the angel of the LORD* was often used in the Old Testament to describe the presence of God Himself.

Boldness is a natural by-product of walking in the light and believing in God's protection. Solomon said it this way: "The wicked man flees though no one pursues, but the righteous are as bold as a lion" (Proverbs 28:1).

Receiving the Lord's Provision

Taste and see that the LORD is good; blessed is the man who takes refuge in him. Fear the LORD, you his saints, for those who fear him lack nothing. The lions may grow weak and hungry, but those who seek the LORD lack no good thing.

Psalm 34:8–10

Everyone who will be mightily used of God must learn that all the things we depend on to succeed—jobs, customers, donations—are only vehicles that the Lord uses to meet our needs. God is our source. David refers to the fact that even lions may grow weak and hungry with age; even the king of the jungle has limits to his ability to provide for himself. In contrast, the believer who fears the Lord will lack nothing. In Psalm 37, David makes this statement more emphatically: "I was young and now I am old, yet I have never seen the righteous forsaken or their children begging bread" (verse 25).

The Power of Positive Proclamations

Come, my children, listen to me; I will teach you the
fear of the LORD. Whoever of you loves life and desires
to see many good days, keep your tongue from evil and
your lips from speaking lies.

Psalm 34:11–13

What you say is what you get! Too many of us do
not understand this point. Solomon summarized all of
David's teaching on words this way: "From the fruit of
his lips a man is filled with good things as surely as the
work of his hands rewards him" (Proverbs 12:14).

Here in Psalm 34, David zeroed in on the relational or
social power of our words. We can build up or destroy
reputations by the words we use. If we use our words
poorly, we will hurt people by lies, criticism and character assassination. If we want the Lord's provision and
blessing, we must learn to rein in our unruly tongues.

Pursuing Probity or Integrity

The LORD is close to the brokenhearted and saves those
who are crushed in spirit. A righteous man may have
many troubles, but the LORD delivers him from them all;
he protects all his bones, not one of them will be broken.
Evil will slay the wicked; the foes of the righteous will
be condemned. The LORD redeems his servants; no one
will be condemned who takes refuge in him.

Psalm 34:18–22

The word *probity* speaks of integrity and personal
honor. When David contrasted righteousness and wickedness, he showed us the advantages of a consistent,
principled walk with God. The Lord will redeem or
deliver those who have chosen to walk with personal

integrity based on His Word. Humility is also alluded to here—as one of the driving forces that help keep us on track.

Soothing Balm for the Wounded

David's men started out distressed, in debt and discontented. On the surface, they would hardly have been described among the most likely to succeed. Very few people would have bet on their futures. Their leader could easily be equated to a fugitive on today's FBI's Most Wanted list. Nevertheless, impressively, David, the shepherd boy turned decorated hero, became a rebel general with the style of Napoleon and tactical ability of Francis Marion—"the Swamp Fox" of Revolutionary War fame.

Later in Israel's history, God would speak of Adullam as a place that would receive "the glory of Israel" (see Micah 1:15). Most scholars believe that this title was conferred on the cavernous terrain because of the exploits of the leaders developed under David. Like a championship coach or a world-class dance instructor, David could spot a diamond in the rough. He knew just how to work with men to bring out their strengths.

Underlying David's world-class coaching ability was a strict code of ethics and principles upon which he had built his life. With that foundation he succeeded in transferring his knowledge of God to those who followed him. As he inspired them to live in earnest relationship with God, they, in turn, found relief from their wounds on many levels and literally transformed the heart, soul, mind and strength of David's army. It was their walk with God that allowed them to do great exploits in combat. In the next chapter we will talk about three of the greatest of these men. Before we move into the next chapter, let's take a moment to review what we have learned in this one.

TAKING INVENTORY

1. Reflect on your "racial history." Were you taught to be biased or inclusive in your early years? What factors have helped you develop your principles in terms of race relations today?
2. In your experience, have you seen churches try to promote racial or ethnic diversity in contrived ways? Why does this method hurt the Church eventually?
3. According to 2 Corinthians 5:14–16, what is the source of reconciliation between men? Why is it the only source?
4. Considering Paul's ability to cross relational bridges, what bridges have you been able to make to advance the Kingdom of God? Have you had to overcome barriers as Paul did in order to navigate these bridges?
5. David's training is an inspiring manual for us as we work with others. How do your leaders inspire you in the following areas? How do you inspire others in the following areas?
   - Prayer
   - Protection
   - Provision
   - Positive Proclamations
   - Probity

10

Profiles in Courage

David's Greatest Soldiers

Courage is first of the human qualities because it is the
quality which guarantees all the others.

Sir Winston Churchill

What if the rich young ruler had sold everything that he
had and given it all to the poor? You remember him—he
was the man who came to Jesus during His earthly ministry and bowed before Him, asking for eternal life. His
problem was that he had kept the rules of religion all
his life but never really found the Lord. This young ruler
is featured in two major passages of the Bible: Mark
10:17–27 and Luke 18:18–27.

Jesus told the ruler that the only way he could be
assured of going to heaven was to cash in all his resources and give them to the poor. Ironically, this bold
young man went away troubled, yet unable to give up

his great possessions. For centuries the debate about this passage has centered around two questions. The first is: "Why couldn't he just drop the goods and become a wholly devoted follower of Christ?" The second is: "What would have happened to him if he had made this extreme sacrifice?"

Why couldn't he let go? The glitter of celebrity and fortune had obviously snared this young man. Like an idol worshiper challenged to give up his god, this mysterious person missed a major opportunity to walk with Jesus and to receive the greatest of all spiritual rewards— eternal life. The young ruler of biblical fame could not transfer his commitment from money to Christ. He left the presence of Christ an unrepentant worshiper of gold instead of a worshiper of God.

In Jesus' commentary about this encounter, He said that it is easier for a camel to go through the eye of a needle than it is for a rich man to inherit eternal life (see Luke 18:25). Passing through "the eye of a needle" was actually a reference to a particularly narrow entrance into Jerusalem.

Wealthy men coming through this entrance had to unpack their heavily laden camels, have the huge animals kneel down, and guide the animals and their goods to the other side of this difficult entry. Material possessions, which are not seen as the superficial trappings they really are, keep many people out of the will of God.

And what would have happened to the young man if he had given it all up? We can only speculate on how quickly the Lord would have worked in His life, but we can be sure that Jesus would have led him into the unique calling chosen for him from the foundation of the world.

Granted, it might not have been a calling to a life of ease; in fact, probably not. Good soldiers need to be ready to sacrifice even more than worldly goods. A modern-day "rich young ruler" who succeeded where this first-century rich young ruler failed has taught us that lesson.

On Thursday, April 22, 2004, a young American met gunfire from suspected Al Qaeda and Taliban fighters. Ambushed on a hazardous mission in southeast Afghanistan, Pat Tillman made the ultimate sacrifice for his nation—he gave his life. Actually, many people believe he gave his life a full year before he was cut down in battle. Let me explain.

After the September 11 attacks on our nation, Tillman was moved by the national tragedy. He walked away from a $3.6 million professional football contract with the Arizona Cardinals to join the military. He became an Army Ranger in 2003, just one year before his death. How can you justify the death of someone who is 27 years of age? The cause is the message of the sacrifice. Important battles require greater sacrifice.

The White House expressed what many Americans feel about Tillman. They called him "an inspiration both on and off the football field." Former Cardinals head coach Dave McGinnis said that Tillman "represented all that was good in sports. Pat knew his purpose in life . . . he proudly walked away from a career in football to a greater calling."[1]

Spiritual battles may require as much of us in terms of courage and sacrifice as the natural battles do. The remainder of this chapter will talk briefly about the mighty men that David developed at Adullam. Then we will discuss two other modern-day spiritual war heroes who have learned to walk the way of the warrior.

David's Mighty Men

Psalm 133:3 says that whenever there is unity, mutual respect and godly vision, the Lord commands a blessing.

This means that the Lord's grace comes upon us as a group to accomplish something for God. Even though David's team functioned well collectively, the men also knew how to be decisive as individuals. There was a connection with both the Lord and the rest of the group that truly made them special. Let's take a moment to review the familiar words:

> How good and pleasant it is when brothers live together in unity! It is like precious oil poured on the head, running down on the beard, running down on Aaron's beard, down upon the collar of his robes. It is as if the dew of Hermon were falling on Mount Zion. For there the LORD bestows his blessing, even life forevermore.
>
> Psalm 133:1–3

Dwelling together in unity means that men and women are humble enough to serve where they are needed in the Body. While these folks serve in the area of need, they use the skills and gifts unique to their own natural and spiritual DNA. Recently a business book entitled *Good to Great* (HarperBusiness, 2001) by Jim Harris showed how organizations with historically mediocre performances turned themselves around. The ultimate answer is that two kinds of people make the difference. The first group comprises selfless leaders who do what is best for the organization based on vision, commitment and unusual character strength. The researchers call these humble patriarchs "level five leaders." David was a level five leader most of his life, except for his domestic problems, which we have discussed.

The second group that transforms organizations is made of skilled workers. Jim Harris recommends that any type of business or organization should go after the best, most brilliant staff. Once these people are on board, the company should play "musical chairs" until the right people find their way to the right seats.

The Kingdom of God works in the same way. It often takes the Lord a long time to get people settled and for them to be content in their unique callings. Comparison and imitation seem to be the greatest sins of the average person. If I compare myself with others, I will be either lifted up in pride or intimidated by the strengths I see in others. Imitators often believe that they can be successful only if they follow some proven pattern. The problem with imitators is that they squeeze themselves into other people's shoes. The ongoing agony of wearing shoes that don't quite fit is stealing the creativity of an entire generation.

People in David's day had all the problems we have. In the early stages of the army, God brought many unskilled men onto the team. At Adullam (see Psalm 34) and Ziklag (see 1 Chronicles 12), David expanded his team rapidly—in fact, at Ziklag there was a massive recruitment of skilled workers. The Lord sent many people to him and David had to determine what his championship team would look like. His greatest strength as a leader was creating a powerful team atmosphere in which the diverse members worked. Somehow David unleashed both creativity and accountability into the lives of his team—a striking accomplishment.

The core values that made David's army great are listed in 2 Samuel 23.This chapter reads like a formal citation for those receiving medals or decorations. The writer knew that David had accomplished something rare. The men had come into a corporate anointing because of teaching and unity. Thirty-seven men are mentioned in this chapter who deserve honor for courage and commitment. These men are broken up into a couple of different groupings.

The Three

These men were outstanding individuals and soldiers. They were Josheb-Basshebeth, Eleazar and Shammah.

David named Josheb-Basshebeth, a Tahkemonite, chief of the Three. "He raised his spear against eight hundred men, whom he killed in one encounter" (2 Samuel 23:8). We can deduce two things about this man's preparation and character. First of all, he must have practiced his spear techniques vigorously. Just lifting a spear eight hundred times quickly would leave you exhausted. Second, he had to remain vigilant or watchful. These eight hundred soldiers must have attempted all kinds of "moves," but Josheb perceived every attack and was victorious.

The name *Tahkemonite* means "thou will make me wise." Josheb obviously lived up to his surname and set an example for all believers everywhere. We must all prepare, remain vigilant and develop godly wisdom concerning our careers or our current fields of endeavor.

The second of the three mighty men was Eleazar. He participated when "they taunted the Philistines gathered at Pas Dammim for battle. Then the men of Israel retreated, but he stood his ground and struck down the Philistines till his hand grew tired and froze to the sword" (2 Samuel 23:9). Eventually those who had left turned around and came back, but Eleazer had killed so many Philistines that his fellow soldiers only had to carry away the dead. The Lord moved mightily because one man refused to run away. Once again this leader lived up to his name, which means "the Lord is my helper."

The third of the three mighty men was Shammah son of Agee. Once when the Philistines gathered "at a place where there was a field full of lentils, Israel's troops fled from them. But Shammah took his stand in the middle of the field. He defended it and struck the Philistines down, and the LORD brought about a great victory" (2 Samuel 23:11).

Shammah's name means "astonishment." I am sure that he shocked his Philistine opponents by standing his ground in a field of beans. Living up to his name as well, he overcame the odds by the help of God. Each one of us may have our day in the sun—a time in which we rise above the crowd to step into our destinies or turn the tide of history for just a few moments.

The Chief Men

In addition to the Three, David had thirty mighty men.

During harvest time one year, David's men came to meet him at the cave of Adullam; a band of Philistines was encamped in the Valley of Rephaim (the valley of the Giants). David commented that he would love a drink from the well near Bethlehem, where the Philistine army was garrisoned. Three of the thirty decided to make his wish their command. The men took no regard for their lives. They broke through the enemy lines, drew water from the well and brought it back to David.

David was shamed that his desire caused those men to risk their lives. He poured out the water before the Lord because he felt that the water represented the lifeblood of the men under his care. The three men who went to the well were Abishai (son of David's sister Zeruiah), Benaiah son of Jehoiada, and Asahel.

Abishai means "my father is a gift." This man's spiritual strength was bolstered by his heritage. He once saved King David's life by killing a Philistine giant who had threatened him (see 2 Samuel 21:16–17).

The name Benaiah son of Jehoiada means "Jehovah has built." The following passage gives a good idea of this man's heroism:

> He slew two lionlike men of Moab: he went down also and slew a lion in the midst of a pit in time of snow: and he slew an Egyptian, a goodly man: and the Egyptian had a spear in his hand; but he went down to him with a staff, and plucked the spear out of the Egyptian's hand, and slew him with his own spear.
>
> 2 Samuel 23:20–21, KJV

Asahel's name means "God made." This man was swift of foot and later was killed by Abner.

The Mighty Ones of Our Generation

There are many people in our day who deserve to be recognized for their faithfulness as soldiers in our generation. These mighty ones know that the weapons of our warfare are not carnal but mighty through God to the pulling down of strongholds (see 2 Corinthians 10:4). Here are two who come to mind and I mention them here because of the balance they both maintain between using their skills successfully "in the world" and yet remaining in humble service to the Lord. There are many, many thousands more, of course, who are faithful to work where God has placed them.

Justice Leroy Hassell is the Chief Supreme Court Justice for the Commonwealth of Virginia. When we were growing up—he is my first cousin—everyone knew that he would be in civic life or politics some day. He studied at the University of Virginia and then at Harvard Law School. After graduation, he worked for a prestigious law firm. On the side, Leroy served on the Richmond

Public School Board from the time he was 24 or 25. What is most amazing to me is that he is well known at his church—and he serves every Sunday morning as an usher.

Justice Hassell's life adds new meaning for me to these verses from Psalm 84:10: "Better is one day in your courts than a thousand elsewhere; I would rather be a doorkeeper in the house of my God than dwell in the tents of the wicked." Mature spiritual warriors are not impressed with position—they are committed to purpose.

Like Leroy, a member of my church whom I will call Keith is an outstanding usher. Keith is committed. Some Sundays he is at church from the first service until the third. Always brandishing a smile and a helpful attitude, he helps make Hope Christian Church a warm and friendly place. This articulate but unassuming man has just founded his own software company. I was shocked that by the time Keith sat down to talk to me about his dream, he had already raised more than five million dollars to begin his company.

This African-American man is the son of a preacher who believes that the Lord has called him into a marketplace ministry. Gifted in so many ways, Keith has learned in previous positions how to hire staff to compensate for his weaknesses and how to run a "cracker jack" operation. At church he understands the ministry environment, at work he discerns ministry moments and in the marketplace he is pioneering new solutions to management problems.

Time for Analysis

I recently attended the installation service of a pastor I have known for sixteen years. Having served under his father for years, the young man was anxious finally to get a chance to implement his own gift of ministry. Outstanding teachers and preachers from around the country were invited to speak at the service. Many had been to the church on numerous occasions. As each one of the guests ministered from the Word, it was easy to see that they had opinions about the next steps the church should take.

As they spoke, some of their words were like prophetic goads poking and prodding the ministry forward. Even the most "laid-back" ministers could not help letting a few of their own ministry desires bleed through into their advice and projections for the church's future. Those with social or political leanings advocated a social agenda. Counselors had concerns about counselor training. The evangelists saw that the harvest fields were ready. And so on.

This was a time in which the congregation was getting a lot of new information. Now both the church's leadership and membership will have to ask God to help them unite around core values and a clear immediate vision. If they unite and work together, great things will be done.

I find that individuals go through as much self-analysis at major seasons of transitions as churches do. Let's take an inventory, therefore, on whether or not we are being the right kind of leader or follower for our churches. Take the next few moments and think about the kind of legacy you want to leave your church, your family, your job, your community and your friendships. Evaluate your progress toward your most deeply held goals. Finally, decide what kind of warrior you will be known as. It is your own "profile of courage."

Remember, we are partners with those who co-create the future today!

TAKING INVENTORY

1. Looking at the mighty men David led, which do you identify with most and why?
2. Are you currently a leader or a follower in your church? Are you the "right kind" of member? Why or why not?
3. What specific legacy do you want to leave for
   • Your church?
   • Your family?
   • Your job?
   • Your community?
   • Your friendships?
4. What are some of the goals you hold most deeply? How are you progressing toward these goals? Are there steps you need to take to increase your progress in any area?
5. What kind of a warrior do you want to be known as? What will people say that will let you know you have succeeded?

11

Let's Change the World!

Salute to a Champion

David! The name that means "beloved." Few names in the Bible are more familiar to us than this. His name appears nearly eight hundred times in the Old Testament and about seventy times in the New Testament. Like a friend and companion, he shares his joys and struggles, his failures and victories.

In fact, we seem to know more details about his life than any other figure in the Bible. From our days as Sunday school children reenacting his victory over the giant Goliath to our current worship ministries setting his psalms of praise to music, we follow David's exploits with interest through our years and his. He was Israel's finest general, her most celebrated king and God's favorite musician.

When we think of great people, we often think of great character traits and great skills. Last year I was scheduled to meet the famed Nelson Mandela. He is one of my heroes because he took his country through turbulent times without resorting to widespread violence. I also hoped he would autograph an official ballot I had from his first presidential race.

As I prepared for this meeting, I found myself thinking intently about questions I wanted to ask him. Which of his personal gifts was most helpful in building his career? Had he concentrated on public speaking? Coalition building? Public policy? What defining event had revealed his unique role in South Africa? What primary area of his life had God dealt with to catapult him with such grace into groundbreaking regional, national and international levels of leadership?

I was truly disappointed when my meeting with Mandela had to be canceled. I am not sure that I will ever get answers to those questions of how the life of this remarkable man has been shaped over the years.

David, on the other hand, is always accessible. His life is an open book. His character traits and skills have been so exposed and analyzed both by Scripture and extrabiblical sources that he can hide nothing from us. The trick in getting the most out of David's life is knowing what questions to ask.

Judson Cornwall told me on several occasions that I could never have the exact same ministry as someone I admired. I could, however, find out the price that person had paid to develop intimacy with God. If I were willing to pay the same price, I could have the same walk with God as anyone on the planet. If I achieved, for example, the same intimacy with God that David had, it would manifest itself in my life, although in a different way. I will never be the sweet psalmist of Israel, but I might be a more godly minister or speaker or author because of the gateway to intimacy with God that I learn about through David.

The Bible first introduces us to David as the youngest of eight sons of Jesse. Most people believe that he was a little guy with light red hair, raised in a home with strapping bruisers for brothers. Unappreciated and unrecognized in his early years, he was given the thankless task of herding the family's flock of sheep. Little did David know that his almost total exile from the family to care for the sheep was a part of God's master plan for his life. It seems that God can use pain or privilege to develop spiritual hunger within us. David used his long, lonely nights to sharpen his skills with his slingshot and his harp. He also used the solitude to learn to pray and to become truly intimate with the Lord.

David was extremely gifted but he also used his skills to move forward in the destiny that God had given him. He learned principles. And predominantly, these principles made David into a great warrior.

In the pages of this work, we have uncovered these principles. They fall into a natural acrostic for our study—the word *WARRIOR*—making it easy for us to remember the individual points as we go about our daily lives. And not only have we analyzed the principles, but we have also gauged our growth toward our own destinies through checklists and questions designed to penetrate our crusty armor and get to the heart of our beliefs and actions. Application of our principles is important—and it is also easily achieved because the principles I have shared *do* work in real life.

Let's take stock one final time together of each principle and your level of achievement for each one.

W—wealth. What influence do you have through the blessings God has given you? Are you one of God's power brokers? Do you follow the ten commandments of influence?

A—achievement. Are you a success in the Kingdom of God? Have you overcome fear? Do you listen to the right voices?

R—righteousness. Have you allowed your personal righteousness to be noticed or heard in your community? Have you demonstrated Kingdom dominion by becoming an advocate for justice?

R—reflection. Have you reprogrammed your mind in order to grow in your ability to think like Jesus? Have you adopted a biblical worldview? Are you growing in the areas of biblical meditation?

I—intercession. Do you pray with authority? Does your prayer life provide you with a power base to fight your battles?

O—outlook. Do you react negatively to people who antagonize you or do you move in the "opposite spirit"? Are grace and peace the marks of your daily life?

R—reconciliation. Do you provide help for those who are wounded around you? Do you bring healing to relationships that have been broken?

I talked early in this book about the goal of finding the specific role God has given you—your own personal destiny. It is my prayer that as you have pursued the steps to becoming God's warrior, your God-given calling has come more sharply into view. As you continue to observe and respond to the world around you, employing these Kingdom insights, you will have the opportunity to move into a zone of maximum impact.

Then, as you rise like David over human frailties into powerful destiny, you will become a true profile in courage, a mighty man or woman of God—a champion.

Walk with me in the way of the warrior. Together we can change the world.

Notes

Chapter 2: Warriors and Warfare

1. Sun Tzu, *The Art of War*, vol. 3, ca. 500 B.C., trans. Giles, as quoted in *The Greenhill Dictionary of Military Quotes* (London: Peter G. Tsouras, 2000), 502.

2. Erwin Raphael McManus, *Uprising, A Revolution of the Soul* (Nashville: Erwin Raphael McManus, 2003), 54.

Chapter 3: Wealth and Influence

1. http://www.themediadrome.com/content/articles/words_articles/poems_nursing.htm access 4/12/05

2. John F. Kennedy, State of the Union Message, Jan. 11, 1962; quoted in *The International Thesaurus of Quotations*, comp. Eugene Ehrlich and Marshall De Bruhl (New York: HarperPerennial, 1996), 741:32.

Chapter 4: Achievement

1. T. D. Jakes, *Maximize the Moment*, reissue (New York: Berkley Publishing Group, 2001), 62.

Chapter 5: Righteousness

1. See www.MyJewishLearning.com. Tzedakah is also discussed on page 43 of Steven Silberger, *The Jewish Phenomenon: Seven Keys to the Enduring Wealth of a People* (Marietta, Ga.: Longstreet Press, 2000).

2. Silberger, 40.

3. Ibid., 42.

Chapter 6: Reflection

1. George Barna, *Think Like Jesus* (Brentwood, Tenn.: Integrity Publishers, 2003).
2. Ibid., 6.

Chapter 7: Intercession

1. John Cook, comp. and ed., *The Book of Positive Quotations* (New York: Gramercy Books, 2000), 129.
2. Peter G. Tsouras, ed., *The Greenhill Dictionary of Military Quotations* (London: Greenhill Books, 2000), 370:2.

Chapter 8: Outlook

1. Joe Gibbs, *Racing to Win: Establish Your Game Plan for Success* (Colorado Springs: Multnomah, 2002), 113.
2. William Barclay, *The Gospel of Matthew*, vol. 1 (Louisville, Ken.: Westminster Press, 1975), 96.
3. *Enhanced Strong's Lexicon* (Oak Harbor, Wash.: Logos Research Systems, Inc., 1995).
4. Robert G. Torricelli, ed., *Quotations for Public Speakers* (New Brunswick, N.J.: Rutgers University Press, 2001), 28.
5. Torricelli, 30. Abraham Lincoln's response to critics of his unwavering support for the Union.

Chapter 10: Profiles in Courage

1. CNN, http://www.cnn.com, access 4/25/05 (23 April 2005).

Index

Harry R. Jackson Jr. and his wife, Michele, pastor Hope Christian Church, a multiracial, multicultural fellowship in the greater Washington, D.C., area. Their hearts' desire: to help others come into God's destiny through inspiration, instruction and impartation. In the United States and overseas they have conducted *Warrior's Heart* workshops; *In-Laws, Outlaws and the Functional Family* seminars; women's and men's retreats; leadership training; worship conferences; and High-Impact leadership seminars.

Bishop Jackson, author of *The Warrior's Heart: Rules of Engagement for the Spiritual War Zone*; *In-Laws, Outlaws and the Functional Family*; and *The Black Contract with America on Moral Values* and coauthor of *High-Impact African-American Churches*, has recently risen to national prominence through his message of righteousness and justice and its application to government policy. He is chairman of a new national organization called High-Impact Leadership Coalition, a Christian nonprofit association currently educating the nation regarding biblical and moral value issues in key urban areas across America.

Bishop Jackson, a scholar-athlete in high school and college, earned a B.A. in English from Williams College and an M.B.A. from Harvard Business School. For his work in Bible schools and churches domestically and abroad, he was awarded an honorary doctorate of divinity by Christian Life School of Theology. He was consecrated a bishop by the Fellowship of International Churches (FOIC).

Harry and Michele Jackson have two daughters, Joni Michele and Elizabeth.

For bookings, videos, audiotapes or CDs, contact:

The Hope Connection
P.O. Box 505
College Park, MD 20240
(240) 206-0111
email: info@thehopeconnection.org
website: www.thehopeconnection.org

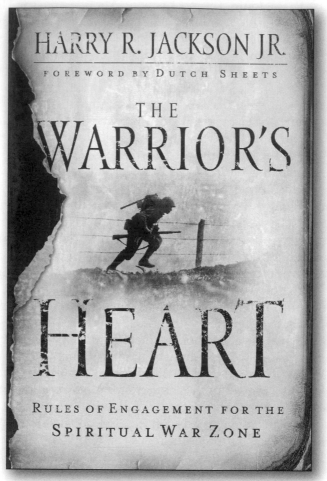